WINTER
SCRAPE

Compiled by Dave Lane

Photo shows aerial view of Rivington Pike with the surrounding tracks. Picture taken by the author from a Mainair Blade microlight.

d.lane@btinternet.com

Second Printed edition July 2008

First Published – Internet edition	*Oct 2003*
1st Revision	*Feb 2004*
2nd Revision	*Oct 2004*
3rd Revision	*Jan 2005*
4th Revision	*Nov 2005*
5th Revision	*July 2006*
6th Revision	*Dec 2006*
7th Revision	*Jun 2007*
1st Paperback Edition A4	*Aug 2007*
2nd Paperback Edition 9 x 6	*Nov 2007*
2nd Edition, Revision 2	*July 2008*

Published & Distributed by Lulu.com
www.lulu.com

©*Dave Lane 2007*

The right of Dave Lane to be identified as the author of this work has been asserted in accordance with the UK Copyright, Design & Patents Act 1988

ISBN 978-1-4092-2068-8

Cover photo: The modern mast on Winter Hill with the original Granada structure next to it. Photograph courtesy of Bill Learmouth who retains full copyright.

To my ever suffering wife Sue, who has endured many absences from home over many years when I've been out "on the hills" - and should perhaps have been at home with the family.

To my two sons, Simon and Richard, who have been dragged on to Winter Hill on many occasions and in all weathers.

To my grandchildren, Megan, Chloe and Ethan who have in turn been dragged onto the hill by their father …… but who all seem to have thoroughly enjoyed the experiences.

To Winter Hill, which will still be there thousands of years after us mere mortals have departed this world. I hope it will provide as much pleasure and interest to future generations as it has to ours.

Introduction.

For what seems like most of my life, I've wandered all over Winter Hill in all seasons and in all weathers. There are many others like me! This bleak and lonely spot somehow pulls us back there time and time again. For those who cannot understand our love and affection for the place, Winter Hill must seem an appalling sort of environment except for on the nicest of summer days! This book is aimed at the "aficionado" but I hope that even the casual reader will be able to get something out of it, if only to see why some of us find the place so fascinating.

This is not a book written entirely by myself. It is a collection of articles, photos, and information about Winter Hill gleaned from all over the place and all put together as a scrapbook. I have gathered this small collection to satisfy both myself and others who are interested both in Winter Hill and the general area.

This scrapbook has been produced mainly for my own interest and will not be "published" or sold in any proper sense of this word. A copy of it (with colour illustrations!) will be placed on the Internet for free download. This printed edition of the book has been made available due to requests from many who have requested such an edition.

Although much of this book has been written by the compiler, some of the material is merely extracts from the work of others. Credits and acknowledgements to the writers are listed in Appendix 1. **The writer receives no royalties whatsoever on this book, and all profits will be donated to Bolton Mountain Rescue.**

At the present time, much of the moorland is bare and desolate. In bygone times this was not the case, so in this publication, older maps (usually from the 1849 edition) have been frequently used to illustrate what the area was like one and a half centuries ago.

No attempt has been made to describe in any great detail the buildings or farms on the lower flanks of the hill as these are all more than catered for in other publications – listed in the Appendix at the end. Even Leverhulmes Terraced Gardens will receive only limited mention for the same reason.

Dave Lane .... November 2007
d.lane@btinternet.com

Where and what?

Winter Hill is an unremarkable, fairly small hill, situated in the North West UK, located near to the towns of Bolton, Horwich, Chorley, and Darwen, on a Western spur of the Pennine range of hills. In this book, the term "Winter Hill" has been deliberately left vague in order to include any adjacent areas of interest!

Winter Hill is marked on Ordnance Survey maps as being a mere 456 meters above sea level - or for those of us who are somewhat older – about 1,498 feet! Local pilots are only too aware of the height of Winter Hill, as the height of the top of the mast at about 2,500 feet tells them that they have only another 500 feet to play with before they are in the airlanes used by the big jets. Now you know why the microlight's fly fairly low over Winter Hill and Rivington Pike!

On a clear day, the view from the top of Winter Hill is quite an eye opener for those who have never seen the view before. Looking

South, the whole of the Cheshire plain is clearly in view with Mow Cop in Staffordshire as the limit. The Welsh mountains are clearly visible to the South West with Snowdon sticking up right in the middle. Anglesey and the Great Orme at Llandudno can clearly be seen. Liverpool Bay, with the Seaforth Cranes at Liverpool (along with the offshore gas rigs) are in view as are Southport (with it's distinctive water tower), Blackpool Tower and we can see North as far as Black Combe in Cumbria. If you have a pair of binoculars handy then take a look Lytham on the Ribble estuary and even the windmill on the sea front can be seen along with the Aerodrome at Warton.

There have always been rumours that on a really clear day (and **really** clear days are very rare) it is possible to see the top of Snaefell on the Isle of Man, around 100 miles away from Winter Hill. Although I have been on Winter Hill in what I would class as the most perfect "seeing" conditions I have, as yet, never seen the Isle of Man from the Hill. I do have poor eyesight! No doubt someone will now contact me to say that they **have** seen the Isle of Man – and if they contact me I'll add that fact to this chapter! *(Since writing this, many HAVE written to say they HAVE seen the IOM!)*

Winter Hill is obviously a relatively "modern" name, as on Speed's map of 1610 and Molls's map of 1724 the given name is "Egberden Hill". As suggested by D A Owen in his booklet "Rivington & District before 1066 AD" the name Egberden Hill is "supposed to have arisen from one of the early kings who hunted in the surrounding forest. The most likely candidate is – Egbert, king of Wessex 800 to 836 AD who by 828 AD had included Northumbria, and therefore Lancashire, in his kingdom". Earlier documents from the 13th century indicate it was called Wintyrhold and Wintyrheld.

The highest point of Winter Hill is marked by the Ordnance Survey Trig point at the edge of the northern escarpment. From time to time this point has been used as the site of a bonfire beacon built and lit at some particular royal occasion – from memory I think the last commemoration beacon was lit in the 1980's to commemorate the 25th anniversary of Queen Elizabeth's reign.

The upper parts of Winter Hill are fairly barren, with poor soil, poor vegetation and with the only visitors being walkers, mountain bike riders, cross country runners, model plane flyers, hang and paraglider pilots, cross country skiers …… and the engineers at the TV station on the summit. A private road does go to the radio mast and in "theory" other traffic is prohibited.

After reading this book, I trust that others may be enticed onto the hill.

++

The Geology of Winter Hill

Winter Hill was not always as it appears today. Once it was not even a hill, nor was it even in the earth's temperate region as it is today. As a result of tectonic plate movements, cataclysmic bending and flexing of the earth's surface and dramatic changes in climate, slowly but surely what we now see today has emerged. Without going into too great detail (unless someone would like to provide me with this detail for inclusion in a later version of this book) a brief description of the Winter Hill geological history follows.

When our planet earth was first formed some 4.6 billion years ago, the earth was in a molten state but slowly started to solidify accompanied by volcanic activity and surrounded by an atmosphere that does not resemble the atmosphere of today. Over billions of years, the earth began to stabilise and life somehow began on our planet. In the Winter Hill area no deep borings have been taken so we have no real record of exactly what lies under our feet at great depth. Closer to the surface however, we do know something about our more "recent" history over the last few hundred million years by studying the geology in mining shafts, shallow borings, quarries etc.

The "upper" portion of Winter Hill consists of a series of layers or seams of sandstones, shales and coal - often referred to as the Millstone Grit, Lower, Middle and Upper Coal Measures. The layers include an endless variety of sediments, coal seams (along with their associated underlying bands of fireclay or ganister) and are approximately 8.000 feet in thickness

This area was once part of the great "Upper Carboniferous" delta of the North of England, a version of some of the more famous world deltas that we have today such as the Nile, Mississippi and Amazon. Somewhere to the north of Winter Hill was a huge land mass with a large river entering the sea (to the South) via a delta. At that stage in the earth's evolution, the surface of the "land" was continuously rising and sinking so the areas near the delta were continuously being raised above sea level, then dropped beneath that level in a succession of floodings and periods when plant growth was possible. Over periods of time, the sandbanks and the muds were overlain with swamps and vegetation only to be inundated over and over again with the either the river or the nearby seas. Thus, over a period of time, the rocks (formed as a result of pressure) have formed in a seemingly endless cycle of marine shales, sandstones, mudstones and vegetative coal layers.

At some stage in the earth's history, the ground underwent tremendous pressures, and parts of our region were bent and twisted due to great internal tensions and this in turn was accompanied by dramatic earth movements where one part of the surface was lifted whilst a neighbouring portion sunk, thus forming "faults". There are a number of faults under Winter Hill. What we now see as the top of Winter Hill was once at sea level covered in lush tropical forests.

For anyone who wants proof of these earth movements I can tell you that it is possible to find fossil remains of those tropical forests (leaves, tree bark and roots, seeds etc) on the very top of Winter Hill ..... they can be found at various points in shale bands on the sides of the road running up to the television mast. Honest! ..... but you'll have to find the sites yourself .... I don't want to be held to blame for new "holes" appearing on the hill top!

There are two main seams of coal under Winter Hill and both have been exploited in the past. In fact, almost the entire section of one part of the south facing flanks of Winter Hill are to all intents and purposes hollow, due to centuries of coal mining, with only pillars of coal being left "in situ" to support the surface as we know it today.

The layers of rock forming Winter Hill are not horizontal but dip towards the south at a dip of 1 in 12. Due to the shape of the hill and the dip of the layers, the upper coal seam is at a fairly constant depth below the surface of the ground despite the fact that the hill is not level!

Apart from Winter Hill providing local people with coal in the past, it also provided stones and rocks for building houses and walls, fireclays and other clays for producing bricks and tiles. Hopefully, this book will provide you with details of all these industries of Winter Hill.

Tigers Clough.

Tigers Clough, or Shaw's Clough as it is usually marked on Ordnance Survey Maps is the wooded valley of the River Douglas which lies a few hundred yards to the north-east of Rivington School. Although today the clough is an oasis of peace, it was not quite so peaceful over a hundred years ago.

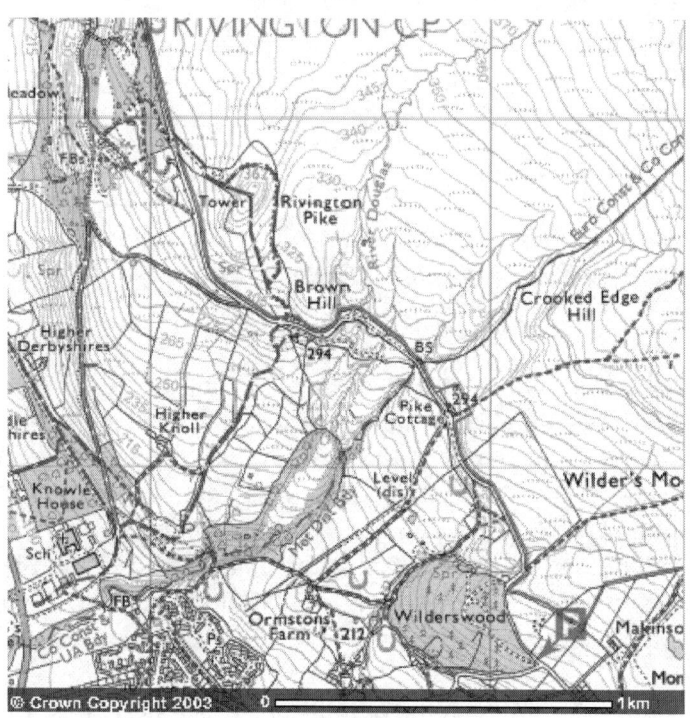

The clough at that time housed a bleachworks, a drinking establishment and with a

brick and pipe works nearby along with a coal mine just higher up the hill. The clough can be best accessed by going up the road to the east of the school to the road junction. Take the concrete road going uphill and opposite the quarry go down the path to the river.

The bleach works mentioned above, was known as Knoll Bleach works and lay on both sides of the river, where some of the remains can still be seen. It was owned by a Thomas Kay and documents indicate that it was used for "rag bleaching". I have no idea what it means, but the works once contained one of the countries first "callenders" which I'm told is some sort of machine that was used to finish off the cloth by putting a glaze onto its surface.

A drawing of Knoll Bleach works from the mid 1800's. I have only a photocopy of this drawing but I am informed that it was drawn in 1849 by a J Whitaker. Source of drawing unknown.

There are conflicting stories about the demise of the bleachworks. One tale tells of a large storm in 1850 which increased the river water levels to such a height that the water wheel and part of the dam were washed away. Another source says that at some time after 1868 Liverpool Corporation had the works demolished as it lay within their catchment area. Both tales may in fact be true with perhaps the works being severely damaged in 1850 and then finally demolished in the late 1860's.

One rather sad story about the bleach works is that in 1798 a local man, John Eccles, was caught breaking into and stealing calico from the works, and in August of that year, he appeared before the Lancaster Assizes and was sentenced to death and executed in September.

Near to the bleach works (believed to have been just downstream from it below the footbridge) and owned by the works owner, there was an alehouse managed at one time by a Mr Brindle. This seems to have been no ordinary alehouse for it was not only unlicensed but sold mainly illegally brewed alcoholic drinks (it was known locally as a "hush shop"). Mr Brindle was obviously not afraid of offending the authorities, for he commissioned a local artist to paint a sign for the drinking establishment and this sign was decorated with the heads of two tigers. This is believed to be why the clough is locally referred to as Tigers clough and not by its "official" name of Shaw's clough!

On the south-western side of Tigers Clough was located the large pipeworks owned by the Crankshaws (also known as "Klondyke") which used the locally mined fireclay in the manufacture of some of it's products. A tramway ran in the fields to the east of Tigers Clough bringing the fireclay direct from the mine level (located in the fields below Sportsmans cottage) straight into the pipeworks. A photo of the mine entrance can be found in one of the mining articles in this scrapbook.

Crankshaw's pipe works, Horwich.

Mankind has always seemed to be attracted to Tigers Clough! In the 1940's a local man was out walking when he spotted an unusual piece of stone in the river. When he retrieved it, he found that it was a six inch long axe head which had been highly polished. At a later date the axe was found to be made of a type of stone found in Scandinavia and was dated to the Neolithic period around 2,500BC.

A walk up the clough is a delight at any time of year, each season bringing it's own sights. The wild flowers, the trees, the ferns and mosses along with the birds and animals make it a pleasure to visit. A trip up the stream from Rivington School to the Pike area, makes an ideal introduction to the geology of Winter Hill and a separate article is included in this scrapbook on a geological trip up the Clough which explains all that can be seen.

Just above the remains of the bleachworks, are two attractive waterfalls, best observed after heavy rain. Just above the waterfalls on the right hand bank, is a very odd shaped rock. The rock has been hand carved with a pick or chisel (the marks are clearly visible) in the shape of a bowl, basin or bath but the purpose of it quite defeats me! One assumes it may be something to do with the bleachworks but the size of the basin makes this somewhat unlikely. Anyone any ideas?

Although it IS possible to walk almost the whole length of the clough in the river bed, unless you are wearing wellingtons or prepared to get wet, this is not recommended, especially as the rocks are extremely slippery in some areas.

Tigers Clough is well worth a visit at ANY season of the year.

Later on in this Scrapbook is reprinted a geological walk which was written some time ago in a booklet published by Wigan Geological Society. It details a walk from Rivington School right up to the Pike via Tigers Clough explaining the geological things of interest to see on the route.

■■■

The unusual shaped "bowl" just above the waterfall in Tigers Clough

The Distant Past on Winter Hill.

People have been visiting Winter Hill for over 4,500 years. Although today, the hill is bare and fairly desolate, apart from the lower slopes, things were not always like this. From the techniques of "pollen analysis" and "pollen dating", it is possible to build up a fairly complete picture of what Winter Hill must have been like over the past few millennia. At some stage I am hoping to obtain detailed information about pollen analysis in the area, and this will be included in the scrapbook.

What is known, is that the top of the hill was not always as bare as it is today. It was once covered in woodland and there is no reason to suppose that perhaps people even lived up here amongst the woodlands thousands of years ago. There is ample evidence on and around the hill to prove that people lived in the area, even though no remains have been found of a true settlement on the top of the hill. The people of the area did however leave remains and artefacts which tell us a little about their existence.

We know for example that men worked on Winter Hill, owing to the finding of a stone axe in Tigers Clough, and the many flint chipping sites which have been discovered on the top of the hill. Flint does not naturally occur in this area, and the early inhabitants of the area (between about 2,000 BC and 1,000 BC) obviously traded with people in other parts of the country in order to obtain the natural flint.

Flint was used for many purposes. We know it was used to fashion arrow heads for hunting, axes for cutting, "scrapers" for dealing with animal hides, knives, and many other articles. We think that the trade in flint comprised of the "purchase" (probably by way of barter) of nodules or lumps of the material, and that the implements were made locally. This theory is backed up by the finding of several small areas of flint "chippings" or "flakes" on the hill, where men would have obviously spent some considerable time "working" on the raw flint, turning it into usable implements.

Probably the "earliest" find in the Winter Hill area is the stone axe that was discovered lying in the bed of the river Douglas in Tigers Clough by a Mr Southworth of Anderton, The axe was about six inches in length and was highly polished and after expert advice had been obtained, it was found that the stone probably originated in Scandinavia and was from the period around 2,500BC. To my knowledge this is the earliest item ever found on Winter Hill.

The only other early remains found on the hill are the two "burial mounds" discovered near the peak of the hill, both thought to date from around the Bronze Age, and indicative that somewhere in the area was a settlement (or settlements) dating from this era.

The first burial mound to be found was the one now known as the Winter Hill Tumulus or Barrow which was discovered purely by chance when John Rawlinson and Tom Creear were walking on the moors in 1957. On the 24th March they spotted what appeared to be a "curved line of stones" sticking out from the peat. The stones were part of a "wall" some two feet in height, which surrounded a round area with a raised small mound in the middle of it.

In July of 1958 a group from Manchester University excavated the central mound but soon discovered that the site had been previously excavated (probably about 250 years earlier). A positive pollen dating showed that the site originated in the Middle Bronze Age round about 1,500BC.

Higher up the hill and on the southern heading edge, lies Noon Hill, upon which is the Noon Hill Saucer Tumulus. Although this had been known to exist for some time it was not until August 1958 that it was excavated. This was undertaken by the Bolton & District Archaeological Society and when the topsoil of part of the site was removed, it revealed two rings of stones one inside the other, the outer ring being about 52 foot in diameter and the inner one 32 foot. The outer wall consisted of "large stones" each about two foot six inches long, a foot wide and eight inches high. The inner circle of small stones were said to have been "strengthened with buttresses".

Inside the inner circle, were two piles of human remains, and nearby was found what is thought to be a cremation urn. I have been unable to find out if there was anything found inside the urn. Also discovered in the tumulus were two barbed flint arrowheads along with a flint knife. All discoveries are housed in Bolton Museum and have been on public view from time to time. So far as I am aware, no pollen dating took place on the Noon Hill Site, but examination of the items found, indicates a date of around 1,100BC for the burial mound.

Various flints "chippings", "flakes" and flint implements have also been found on the moors but I have unfortunately never managed to find the exact locations. Some 15 to 20 years ago, I remember seeing a map showing the sites of all the flint "finds" on the Hill (it was pinned to the wall of the head rangers office in Middle Derbyshires Farm) but I have never managed to trace a copy of the map since that time. If anyone **has** a copy of the map PLEASE get in touch with me and if I can get permission, I'll put a copy in this scrapbook!

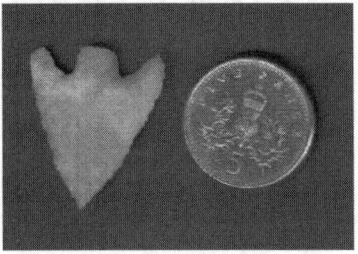

I find it particularly galling and frustrating, for although I have tramped and searched on Winter Hill for almost 30 years, I have never even found so much as a single flake of flint on Winter Hill -

even though other individuals have found dozens! The only flint I have **ever** found in the locality, was a superb barbed arrowhead (minus shaft) found some 20 yards due north of the peak of Black Hill on Anglezarke Moor and is illustrated below.

++

The Winter Hill Mass Trespass of 1896.

It is not widely known that a mass trespass took place on Winter Hill in 1896 nearly 50 years before the more famous mass trespass on Kinder Scout in 1932. It was the response of the people of Bolton to the closure of footpaths and roads over Winter Hill by the landowner Colonal R H Ainsworth JP of Smithill's Hall, in order to protect his grouse shooting.

The demonstration followed much controversy and demands for an enquiry, which were resisted by Col. Ainsworth. The organisers called on the people of Bolton to join them in a walk from Smithill's Hall, along the disputed Coal Pit Road track to Winter Hill on Sunday 6th September 1896. Over 8,000 turned up!

They were addressed by several speakers and the organisers asked the walkers to keep to the path and not trespass on the surrounding land. Upon reaching the disputed track, the walkers were confronted by a fastened gate plus a group of police and men who were employed by Col Ainsworth. The walkers jumped over the gate that blocked their path, eventually knocking it down and they uprooted the "Trespassers Will Be Prosecuted" notice, throwing it into the ditch to loud cheers. They also knocked over a police inspector.

After passing through Col. Ainsworth's land the route passed onto land leased by Mr Deakin of Belmont Bleach works, who since 1893 had been trying to close the Belmont to Rivington road over the moors. When viewed from the summit of Winter Hill it was reckoned that the procession was over 1.5 miles in length.

The following Sunday, the 13th Sept another walk was organised and this time it was estimated that 12,000 people took part. They met at the junction of Blackburn and Halliwell roads and marched to Smithill's Hall then up and over the moors again. This time the 60 police present who were positioned where the gate had been were more conciliatory and the gates no longer blocked the path.

The demonstrators were aware that they ran the risk of being prosecuted for trespassing, which would be very serious for ordinary working people would be unable to pay the fines which may have been levied and they might well lose their jobs if found guilty of an offence in court.

Col. Ainsworth did in fact pursue the question of access in the courts, seeking an injunction to restrain over 30 people and through them, the general public, from passing over his land. He also claimed damages.

When his case came to court in Manchester in March 1897, judgement was given in his favour with costs being awarded against the defendants.
(this article appeared as an information panel at the Rivington Visitor Centre).

The major local hill summits within the Winter Hill area.

Adam Hill		
Brown Hill	325m	1066 feet
Brown Lowe	325m	1066 feet
Burnt Edge	325m	1066 feet
Counting Hill	433m	1421 feet
Crooked Edge Hill	375m	1230 feet
Egg Hillock	328m	1076 feet
Noon Hill	380m	1247 feet
Rivington Pike	362m	1188 feet
Two Lads	389m	1276 feet
Whimberry Hill	340m	1115 feet
White Brow	358m	1175 feet
Winter Hill	456m	1496 feet

The Origin and Development of the Moorland.

(Sections of this article are taken from one of the information panels in the Rivington Visitor Centre and are reproduced with their permission)

Winter Hill – and the surrounding upland areas – have not always been as bare and empty as they now appear. At one time they were forested and contained many different types of trees and bushes as has been proved by pollen analysis and pollen dating tests done on the moorland. So what happened to change things?

The process of deforestation started as soon as human settlements began in the area. The natural resources provided by the forest provided building materials, fuel and to a lesser extend food for the settlements. Early inhabitants may have cleared extensive areas of forest around their settlements for simple agriculture. Demands for more basic materials and increased areas for agriculture would have led to a joining up of clearings to create large open tracts of moorland. One pollen analysis investigation of Winter Hill showed a clearly defined woodland clearance of the area in the Norse period, followed by considerable woodland regeneration thought to be through the Middle Ages. It is possible that the original clearance could have been earlier, perhaps even Roman, but I have as yet not managed to get hold of the carbon datings that were carried out at Harwell for this investigation. Pollen analysis was also carried out in the 1980's at Round Loaf Tumulus, Black Brook and Pikestones as well as on Winter Hill. The Winter Hill measurements were taken at SD 627 172 at a profile depth of 1m 46cms.

Grazing.
Probably the single most important factor in the development of these man made moorlands was the introduction of grazing livestock, particularly sheep. Sheep will nibble almost any vegetation down to ground level thus preventing the generation of tree species. Continual grazing by sheep alone will, in time, convert a woodland into a moorland. The practice of running large flocks of sheep on the moorland has not only contributed to the deforestation but has maintained a virtually treeless landscape.

Fire.
Fire would have played a part in the reduction tree cover. Fire can occur naturally in a forest due to lightening strikes and it can devastate large areas. In the years following a forest fire there is usually an increase in the seedling growth of "pioneer" species such as the fast growing birch, willow and rowan. These in turn provide shelter for the slower growing and less numerous species such as oak, ash and pine. Over a long period of time the character of the forest would be restored. Should fires occur on a frequent basis or grazing of livestock be established then the pioneer species would be prevented from regenerating ultimately causing the death of the forest and the creation of moorland.

Today, periodic burning is part of moorland management. The intention is to burn off the mass of dead vegetation from previous years and encourage early growth of grasses for the grazing livestock. Given the right conditions, controlled burning will remove the dead vegetation without damaging the plant roots and the resulting ash will return much needed minerals back into the soil. However uncontrolled fires due to accident or vandalism can over a period of years have a detrimental effect on the mix of moorland vegetation, leading to a loss of habitat for insects, birds and mammals and it reduces the value of grazing moorland for livestock. In severe cases it can also result in the burning of the underlying peat (sometimes to a great depth) leading to the complete loss of all vegetative cover.

The soil or peat.
As if mankind has not done enough damage to the moor, nature has not helped either in latter times. The rocks of the area tend to be Millstone Grit, a rather rough form of Sandstone. Soil is usually formed both by the weathering of rocks and the rapid breakdown of vegetation which in theory should provide good soil along with the nutrients necessary for plant and tree growth over a period of time. Unfortunately Millstone Grit breaks down mainly into rather rocky sand with little nutrient content and the high rainfall on the moorlands washes out most of the other nutrients. These factors combine and peat begins to form which in turn makes the land acidic

in which many plants just will not grow. Thus we have Winter Hill as we have it today!

Moorland Plants of Winter Hill.
I'm not a botanist and I had rather hoped I'd be able to persuade someone else to write this section (any offers?) so for present you're stuck with my rather simplistic explanations as to what grows on Winter Hill!

There are two major types of grasses, purple moor grass *(Molinia Caerulea)* and wavy hair grass *(Deschampsia flexuosa)*. Purple moor grass is very common throughout the UK and is often the dominant grass on damp moors, heaths and fens around the country. It's perennial and forms tufts or tussocks with the flowerhead usually dark purple (but occasionally pinkish, yellowish or green). In height it varies from 15 to 100cm and flowers between July and September. This is the "ankle breaker" on parts of Winter Hill forming large tussocks, which are partially obscured by the long flowering stems in summer – and this period they are a curse for the hayfever sufferer. The other variety of grass common on the hill is the wavy hair grass but this forms smaller tussocks and flowers in June and July forming delicate heads appearing like a pink mist on the ground. This is the commonest grass on the moorland in the area. The only other major type of grass found on the hill is mat grass *(Nardus Stricta)*, a hard & fibrous grass growing between 10 and 40 cm in height forming dense tufts. This is unpalatable to sheep.

One type of grass seen in many of the damper areas of Winter Hill is cotton grass *(either Eriophorum vaginatum or Eriophorum angustifolium.* This is instantly recognised by everyone with its white tufty cotton like flowers between April and June and it grows only on wet ground.

There are also a number of sedges and rushes on the hill (you can tell the difference between grass and sedge easily enough, in cross section grasses are round and hollow whilst sedges are triangular). I haven't got a clue about the names of the sedges on Winter Hill so if there are any knowledgeable botanical readers out there then please get in touch – or write a full article for inclusion in the next update.

Rampant on parts of the moor is bracken *(Pteridium aquilinum)*, and probably the best known fern, unfortunately it is also one with the most nuisance value as a weed. It can be poisonous to livestock if eaten in quantity but is normally avoided by cattle, sheep or rabbits and so it spreads in their grazing areas fairly rapidly thus reducing the value of the land for grazing purposes. The far reaching underground rhizomes makes eradication difficult. This plant dies away every winter and what might have been a pleasant place to walk at that time of year can become a nightmare in mid summer – especially when it's wet! Bracken only thrives on dryish ground.

Also found on Winter Hill is heather and a similar plant called crowberry. Bilberry *(Vaccinium myrtillus)* is also rampant in some areas and makes delicious pies if you have considerable time to spare, collecting the fairly small berries. A good area for bilberry is to the west of Wilderswood and around the quarries at the northern end of Scout Road.

I'm not going to disclose the exact location, but on the top of Winter Hill is a fairly large patch of cranberry.

In many areas on the hill sphagnum moss grows in profusion both in small patches and in raised bog areas. Sphagnum is unique in that it can hold vast quantities of water even in dry seasons, some varieties holding more than others. Also on the moor are quantities of mosses, lichens and ferns. One day I really must get around to learning what they are all called.

The story behind the Stump.

Scotsman's Stump is the name given to a gaunt iron pillar on the top of Winter Hill located directly in front of the TV station. The "stump" is topped with a plaque, which states "In Memory of George Henderson, traveller, native of Annan, Dumfrieshire who was barbarously murdered on Rivington Moor at noonday November 9th 1838 in the 20th year of his age".

One of the best descriptions of what happened that November day can be found in M D Smiths excellent book "About Horwich" (I understand that another excellent description can be found in the booklet "Murder in the Heather" by David Holding – published in 1991 by the Friends of Smithills Hall). I'll try to give a potted resume but I have to admit that most of my facts came from Mr Smith's book

Poor George Henderson was a young man of 20 who earned his living as a travelling packman or salesman, who sold goods in the area for his Blackburn based employer. He obviously travelled the same route with great regularity, for every other Friday he would meet another packman and the two would meet at Five Houses beer house on the moor and then travel together back to Blackburn. On this occasion George Henderson never turned up for the usual meeting.

His body was found on the hilltop, having suffered severe gunshot wounds. There were a number of people on the moor that day, some of whom reported the presence of a man carrying a shotgun in the area where Mr Hendersons body was found. The man seen was said to be James Whittle, a 22 year old collier who by coincidence lived in one of the "Five Houses" on the moor.

Whittle was arrested and stood for trial at Lancashire Assize courts but was found not guilty by the jury and was therefore discharged.

The exact site of the murder was at the side of the road opposite the main entrance to the television station located at the top of Winter Hill, and originally a tree was planted at the spot as a memorial to George Henderson. In 1912, the tree was removed and replaced by an iron post and plaque.

The Mines of Winter Hill

Winter Hill, especially on the southern side, was once extensively mined for coal. The coal mining activities were so great that that the higher slopes on the Horwich side of the hill are virtually "hollow" except for pillars of coal that were left "in situ" in the mines to stop total roof collapse.

Mines on the Hill included, Montcliffe Colliery, Mountain Mine, Wilderswood and Wildersmoor Collieries, Burnt Edge Colliery, Winter Hill Mine and many other smaller enterprises. The coal seams outcropped at various places on the hill and initially local people would dig away at these points to hew easily obtainable fuel, both for personal use and for sale. Many of these enterprises may have been only one man digging on his own, but others may have been groups of men or a family working on the outcrop. Many of these mines were probably only of small size and would soon be abandoned because of air problems, flooding, roof collapse or other reasons. Because of the small nature of these workings, there is little obvious evidence of this type of working left on the moor.

Once the location of the coal seams were known, small shafts would have been dug to intercept the coal under the surface. These diggings were in the form of "bell pits", so called because the shaft would be dug to the seam then the coal extracted at each side of the shaft forming a bell shaped hole. Once the coal was extracted, another shaft would be dug nearby and in some areas around Horwich whole groups of these pits can be found. There are the remains of some bell pits to the east of Rivington Pike.

Apart from the outcrop workings, the bell pits, and the major commercial undertakings, there were also a number of "trial" workings on Winter Hill, some of which produced small quantities of coal and others which were soon abandoned. The workings to the west of Rivington Pike fall into this category - and one of these shafts is described in this article.

Some of these mines and coal workings will be described below, but readers will have to excuse the lack of exact or precise details of some of the mines due to the dangers inherent in any coal mines. Take my word for it, roof collapses are **not** uncommon, some coal mines **do** contain gases, they **can** be **very** dangerous places. Don't even **think** of going inside old coal mines. All of the underground photographs in this article, were taken by experienced people fully equipped with all the latest safety equipment and mining safety technology. The mines under Winter Hill are particularly dangerous because "pillar and stall" working was practiced in the whole area and the underground workings are rather like a maze on a massive scale, with square miles of passages entered via only one entrance/exit. One's chances of getting lost are pretty high, and apart from going into the "entry" points and pottering near those entrances, the writer has NOT explored the mines even though I was with fully equipped groups.

1. Mining remains near Rivington Pike.

The area around the Pike contains a number of mining remains, shafts, adits and spoil heaps but very little remains today except surface markings. The shafts and adits have long since been filled in.

Very little documentation exists about these mines and what little does exist, is not very explanatory or informative. The only entrance open in recent times has been a shaft which first opened up about 15 years ago following severe storms on the moorland. This was located on the moor behind the pigeon tower, on the banks of the stream just above the water tank. Due to the dangerous nature of this shaft (and one on the opposite bank) they were quickly filled in by the Coal Authority. No records were made of the shafts, no photo's were taken nor were any measurements made.

A couple of years ago one of the shafts re-appeared and was quickly explored. The shaft was very unusual in that it contained a short series of steps carved into the side near it's entrance, it being the only known example of this in the area. A very poor quality photo is shown below with the steps visible on the right hand side.

Other photo's were taken within the shaft but it was very wet and muddy, and the extreme condensation on the camera made the pictures unusable. At the bottom of the steps, the tunnel continued for only a very short distance before being blocked by glutinous mud. Two plans exist of mining remains in this immediate area and

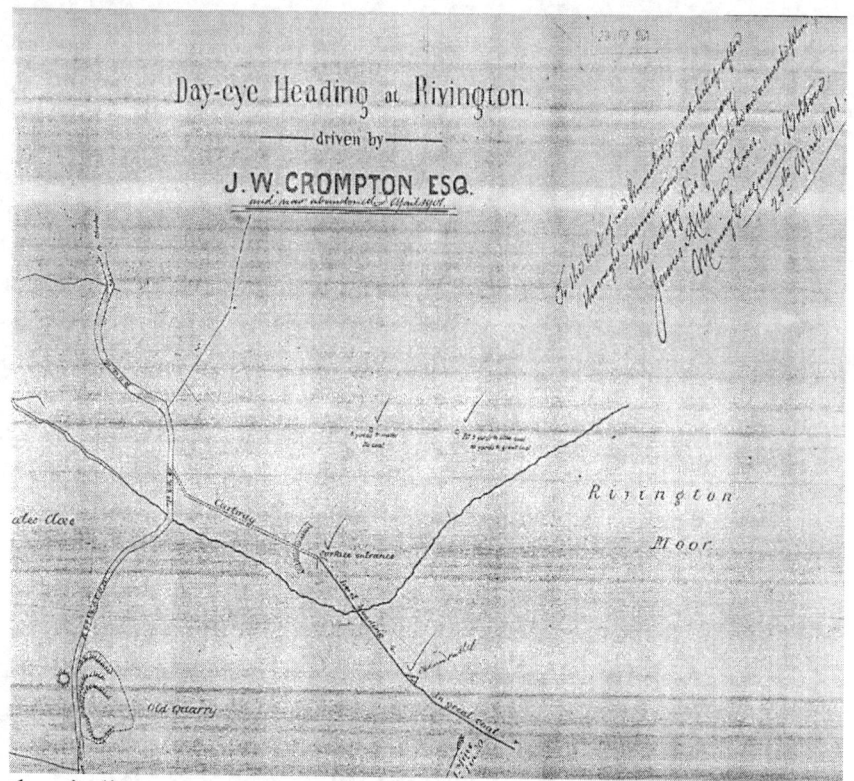

they indicate that the tunnel went only a short distance. The shaft was soon filled in by the authorities before proper measurements could be taken.

The filled in shaft on the opposite bank was filled in years ago. My memory has it that this shaft was much deeper than the earlier mentioned one and had a ladder sloping deeply down on one side of it. If anyone else has memories of this shaft, further details would be appreciated.

Further down the hill heading towards the moorland road is a small pile of mining spoil. This marks the entrance to the drift mine which led into the coal workings. The drift has long since vanished but its location is clearly shown on old maps. A trackway led from the tunnel entrance down to the road.

The map below shows the drift entrance. The quarry behind the Pigeon Tower is in the bottom left hand corner of the map.

2. Montcliffe Colliery, Horwich.

The colliery was located on the north side of Georges Lane above the Mill at Wallsuches and lay behind the row of houses at the hamlet of Moncliffe.

There were two shafts at the mine, numbers 1 & 2. The number 1 shaft later became the main hauling shaft with number 2 being used as an air shaft, following the use of the mine for water extraction purposes - providing drinking water for the town of Horwich (there is a separate article on this subject elsewhere in this publication). Number 1 shaft is 381.25 in depth and number 2 is 429.02 feet

Few photographs exist of the mine but those I have managed to find are produced on this and the next few pages. The first photo shows the number 1 shaft behind the houses. The air or vent shaft is off the photo just to the right of the right hand chimney on the white cottage. The man is believed to be Mr Reg Brownlow.

Number 1 shaft taken around 1960

The number 1 shaft, photo taken around 1966.

The number 1 winding engine at Montcliffe.

So what's it like today underground?

The bulk of the Montcliffe workings were accessible only via the now filled in shafts and so there is no access to these parts of the mine. There is however an adit entrance leading to near the base of one of the shafts and a brief exploration of this part of the mine was made by an industrial history mining group some years ago. This section of the Colliery was known as the Margery Mine.

An initial trip was made into the mine some years ago, and due to the dangerous state of parts of the workings, only one further visit has been made (up till March 2005). This perhaps a shame as it would have been useful had maps been drawn of the tunnels purely for historical purposes. The tunnels explored do not appear on the main Montcliffe Colliery map I have in my possession.

The workings are entered via a long adit which is around 3 foot 6 inches in height. Movement is extremely uncomfortable due not only to the low height but also to the pipe which occupies part of the floor space and a sort of crouching crab like shuffle is the only way to progress. The adit is perhaps several hundred yards long (it was not measured - but it felt like several hundred yards from my

recollections). The tunnel is cut through gritstone. A rockfall is encountered which almost blocks the passage but can be negotiated by a crawl underneath some "hanging death" types of rock.

Once through the rockfall, the coal measures are encountered along with an entrance to one of the main shafts (now fully filled in). I have no recollection of seeing any fire clay either above or below the coal seam at this point and the coal lies directly beneath the sandstone bedding plane. The coal seam is around 3 foot in thickness.

The condition of the passages within the coal seam are generally good, although in some areas the sandstone has shaled off the roof.

Photo showing a miners helmet left underground after the mine closed. The helmet and other items spotted underground have all been left as they were found.

There are a lot of unknowns about this part of Montcliffe Mine. Why was it called Margery Mine? Why does very little coal seem to have been extracted? Why is there a tunnel which just doubles back on itself? All very odd.

I will admit that although I've only been in this mine once, I wasn't too keen on it at all and I left whilst others in the party explored further!

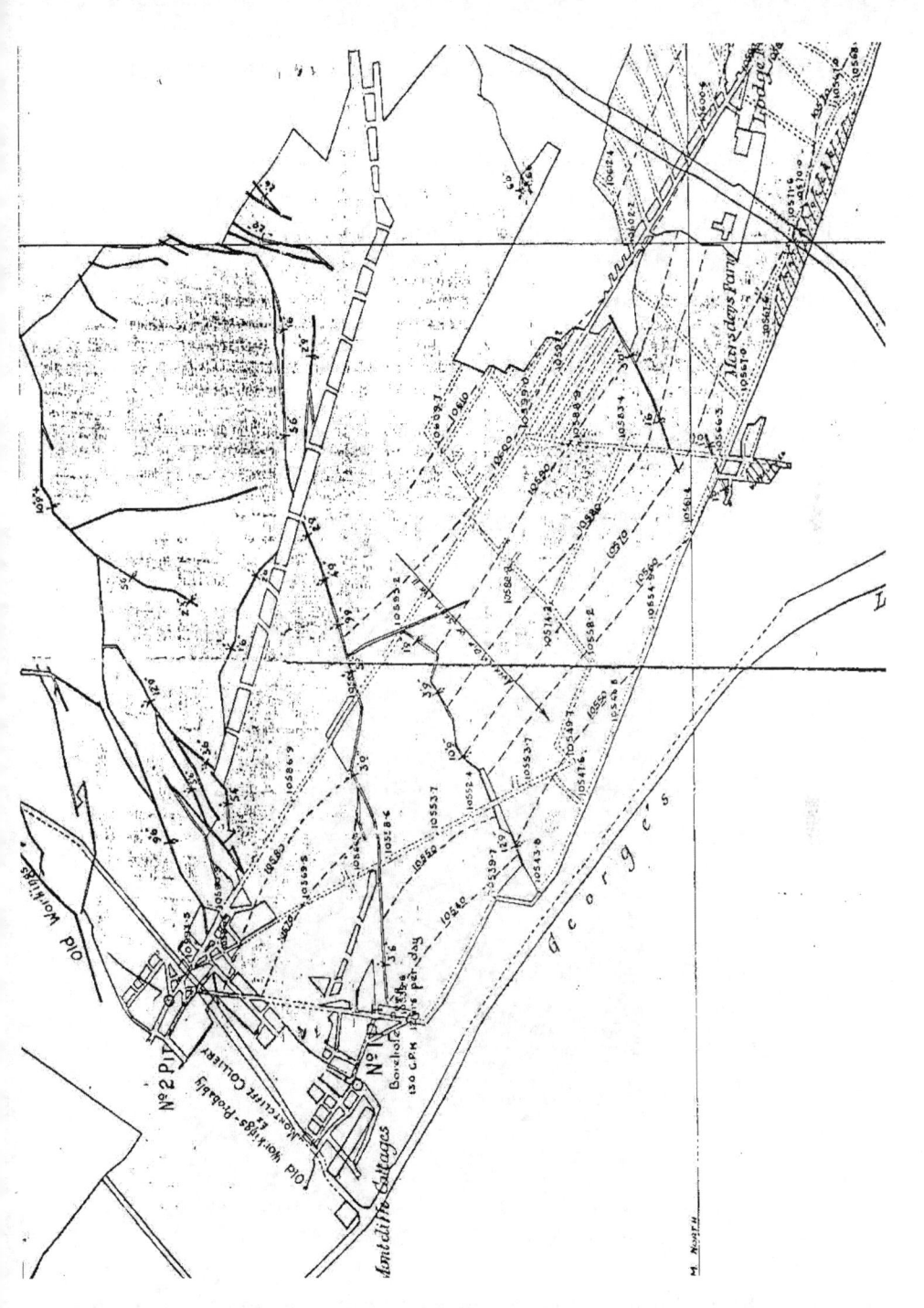

Copy of mine abandonment plan for Montcliffe Colliery dated 1968

3. The Wilderswood & Wildersmoor Collieries.

These mines cover a vast area with a very complex tunnel system in which it would be very easy to get lost. The mines operated on two levels, each working a different seam of coal. The seams are the Little Mine and the Great Mine, with Little Mine being some 25 feet above the Great Mine.

The Wilderswood Drift Mine was privately owned and extracted both coal and fireclay via it's main drift entrance in the fields just below Sportsmans Cottage on George's Lane. The mine ceased operation in 1961 and the drift entrance is now securely blocked.

The main drift entrance, now filled in.

The main rock of the area is sandstone/gritstone and the Little Mine coal seam is only around 10 inches thick but it is underlain with several feet of fireclay which was also extracted for use in Horwich.

The average extraction of material was about 5 feet and the lower levels of fireclay was often left in situ as can be seen in the next photograph.

There were a number of entrances into Little Mine along with some underground links into Great Mine. The entrances were a mixture of adits and shafts but as the coal seams lay only just underneath the surface the shafts were only shallow. All the shafts and adits have been filled in and sealed.

The photo's in this article were obtained only when collapses occurred underground and new temporary entrances appeared on the surface (often widened and shored by the explorers!). It must be stressed that during recent explorations in this mine NO sealed original entrances have been breached whatsoever and entrance has only been gained through new holes appearing on the surface.

There is of course great controversy about the exploration of these mines. The "authorities" do not like people who explore old coal mines and they – quite rightly – have to consider public safety especially in this age of endless compensation claims! Unfortunately in their zeal for public safety, the authorities seem determined to wipe out all evidence and all practical signs of the areas mining history. Indeed in the last few years they have spent tens of thousands of pounds obliterating all signs of mining activity on the top of Winter Hill. Fenced shafts (totally blocked already!) have been bulldozed. Any signs of mining activities have been filled in as quickly as possible. So far as I am aware, no historical records (ie photographs, measurements etc) are being made of the sites prior to their total destruction.

Unfortunately – or fortunately – people other than the "authorities" think differently. They want to know more. They want to know the history of a place. They want to explore that history for themselves. Whilst wishing to abide by the law, they are at the same time, torn by the wish to learn more about the history and they want to explore further. This is not a new phenomenon as the photo below illustrates!

Photo taken in the 1970's prior to an underground exploration of a small tunnel entrance into the Little Mine located in the valley below Two Lads. This photo was deliberately chosen as it is one of the few I have that does NOT show one of the present West Pennine Moor Wardens. Unfortunately it seems to show a leading member of the Bolton Mountain Rescue Team getting kitted out!!!!!!

Whatever the rights or wrongs of the explorations of the tunnels of Winter Hill, I am grateful to those explorers who have let me have copies of their underground photo's so that we can all share in the history of Winter Hill.

Over the past five years, two entrances to the Wilderswood and Wildersmoor complex have been discovered and explored.

One entrance was on the lower slopes of Winter Hill and one was near the top of the hill. The upper entrance (SD 65633 13842) was first spotted on a cold and frosty day when a walker saw steam coming from a small hole in the ground. The steam was obviously warm air coming out of the mine and condensing on contact with the cold air outside. The "team" were alerted, and the small hole was enlarged until easy entrance to the mine tunnel beneath could be effected. A metal lid was used to cover the hole and grass was placed on top. On a later date, the shaft was lined with wood for safety purposes, and a ladder installed, making it easy to enter the tunnels that lay about 8 feet below the surface.

The tunnels radiating from this entrance were explored over the next 12 months but only on a very intermittent basis due to the proximity of public footpaths and roads. Eventually the entrance was discovered by the "authorities" – probably because most of the grass covering the entrance had died and on at least one occasion I found the entrance lid partially off. Due to the presence of bats in the tunnels the entrance was sealed with a concrete surround, topped with an iron grill to enable the bats to enter and exit. Within months, the grills were sawn through by unknown parties and the authorities had no option other than to fill in and completely seal the entrance. There is now no sign of the entrance – nor of the nearby shakehole which some naughty people might have decided to excavate once the main entrance had been sealed! Both have now been totally filled and sealed.

Adjacent to this part of the tunnel system was an area where the coal was extracted in 1960/1 by opencast to recover the pillars of coal left by the earlier mining operations. When the coal had been removed at the opencast, the tunnel entrances in between the pillars were sealed with large timbers and the entrances collapsed and filled with earth and stone. At times in the past, these entrances have been semi-exposed but around 3 years ago the area was totally sealed and covered.

The entrance lower down the hill is still "intact" but the mine is inspected and visited only about twice a year to protect the location and any further comments from me would be inappropriate!

A few more underground photo's are illustrated below and overleaf

……….. but many more can be seen on the Internet at: http://www.d.lane.btinternet.co.uk/winterindex.html

Exploring a timbered roadway in the vicinity of Sportsman's Cottage.

The photo above shows a portion of the mine very near to Two Lads. Roof collapses are evident and have occurred in relatively recent times.

44

An amazing find! The main winding wheel for hauling tubs up the incline from the drift entrance - still intact.

A brick lined section in the lower Wilderswood section ...... and yes ...before you ask ... that is the person you think it is on the right hand side of the photo ... Fred Dibnah is hard to recognise without his flat cap!

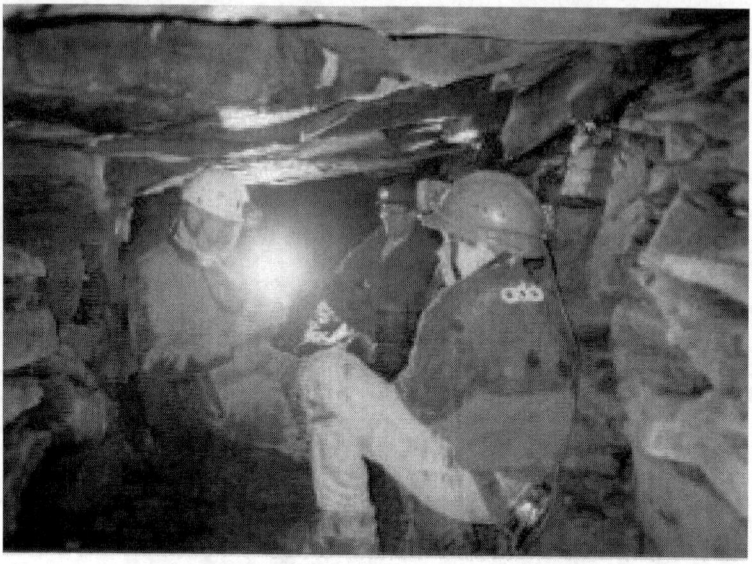

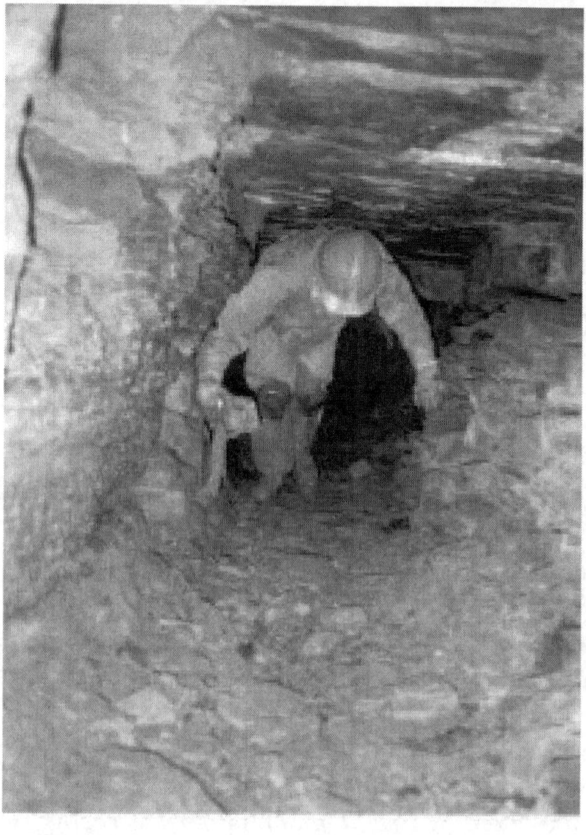

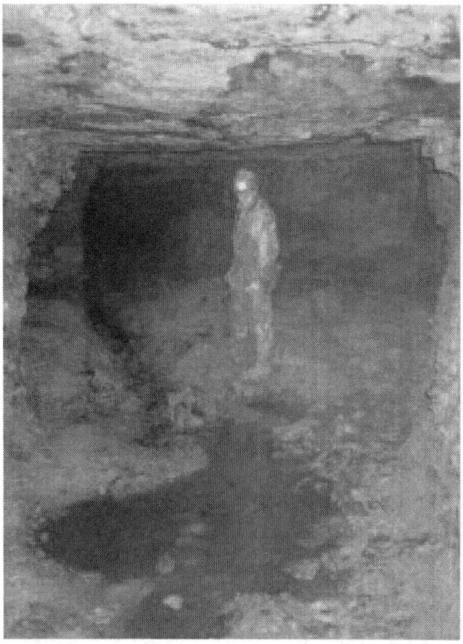

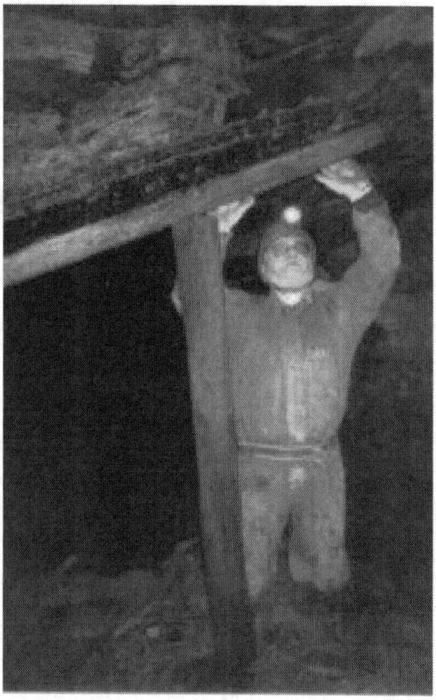

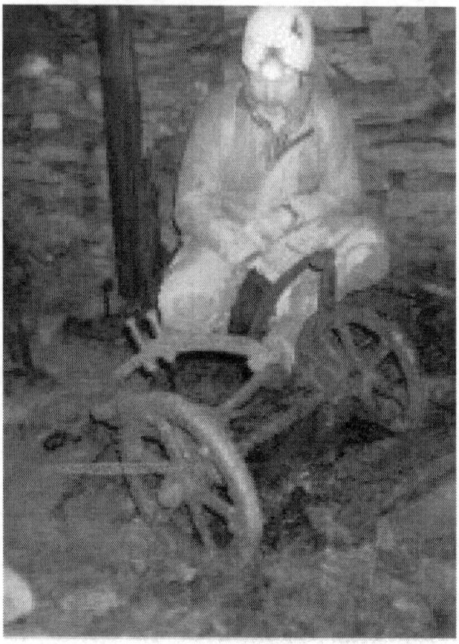

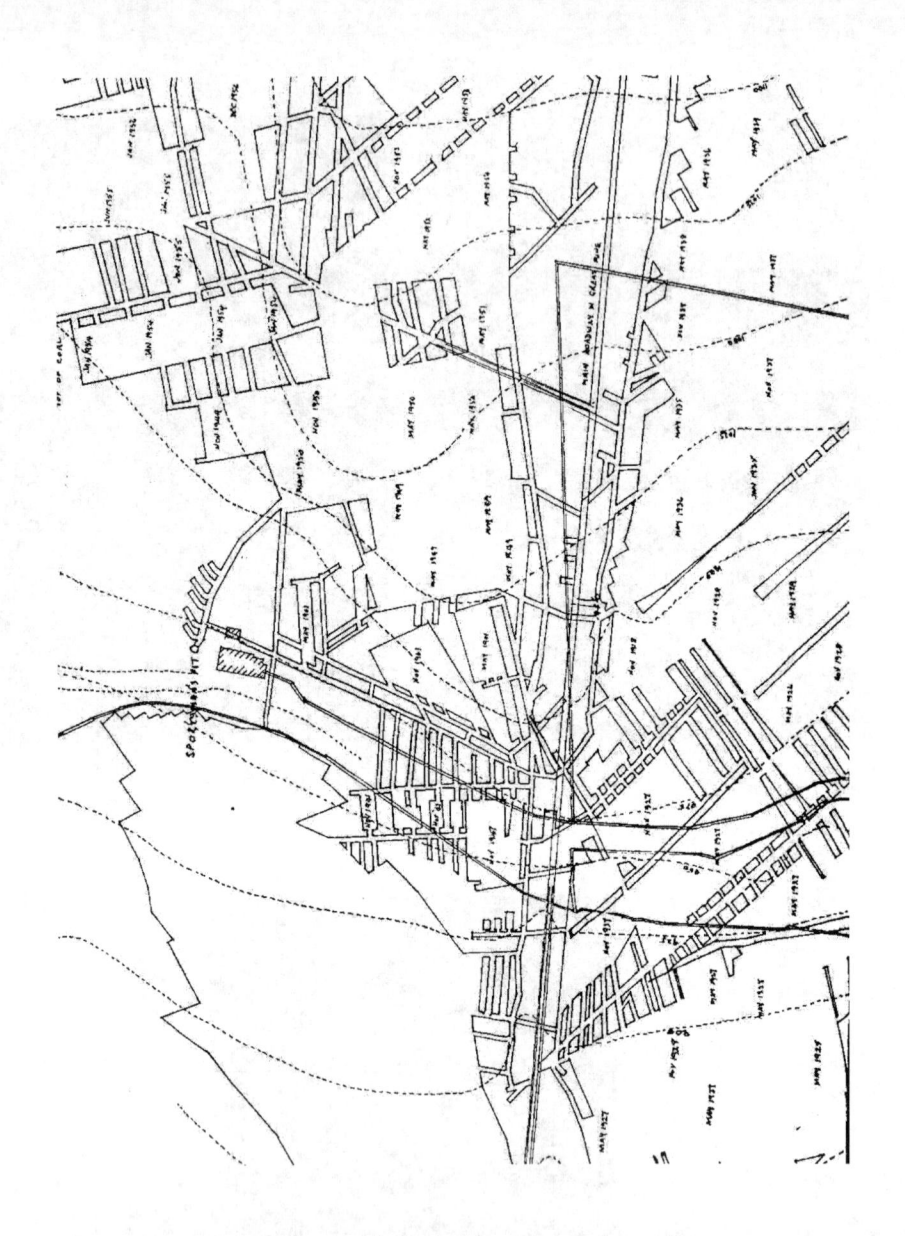

Part of the abandonment plans of a small portion of the mine. This shows the area to the north and south of Sportsman's cottage. The walls alongside George's Lane are indicated by the double lines. The straight tunnel passing through the centre of the map is the main haulage way leading from the drift entrance to the south of the cottage. This tunnel goes right up the hill and ends a few hundred yards south of the TV mast on the summit. The tunnel may in fact be linked to the Winter Hill Tunnel on the other side of the hill but no maps seem to exist of this area and so far, no underground links have been found.

4. Mountain Mine. Winter Hill.

The mine was operated by Messrs J Crankshaw & Co Ltd and opened in 1860, closing in October 1908. The mine was part of "Wildersmoor Colliery" but may have been a separate enterprise from what we **now** refer to as "Wildersmoor Colliery".

Mountain Mine was located mainly to the east side of the road leading to the TV masts on Winter Hill, although considerable workings also extended to the other side of the mast road. The earliest major mining enterprise on Winter Hill apart from small bell pits, outcrop workings and the small coal extraction mines would appear - according to old mining maps of the area - to be those workings entered via the **Winter Hill Tunnel** on the Belmont side of Winter Hill just beyond the masts. It is difficult to determine exactly where the Winter Hill Tunnel "mine" and Mountain Mine started and ended for plans of both mines show common areas of coal extraction. The earliest **recorded** date of coal extraction that I have so far found in the whole complex is 1833.

The total Wildersmoor complex included at least seven major adits or drifts, plus at least nine main shafts and various other air shafts, "pits" and many other smaller entrances (mainly adits) all linking into the system. Many of the coal and clay seams were worked to the surface outcrops. There are no known **open** entrances to the mine. The water authorities seem to have "commandeered" one drift entrance for water extraction purposes. The "Dip" (or angle of gradient) of the workings is 1 in 12 towards the south.

The surface of the moor in this area indicates a massive amount of coal working with bell pits, collapsed tunnels, possible mine entrances, mounds of excavated material etc all over the place. All entrances are completely filled in and sealed (and all have been examined from the surface). From time to time a collapse occurs underground leaving a hole on the surface, but the "authorities" soon fill these in, sometimes within days of them appearing.

I have been unable to locate any early photographs of the Mountain Mine either on the surface or underground. If anyone can help you can contact me at d.lane@btinternet.com

Looking at all the plans of this area it would be safe to say that this whole portion of Winter Hill is hollow and massive amounts of coal and fire clay have been removed over a period of more than 150 years. Most walkers on Winter Hill have no idea of what is under their feet or the hard toil that was carried out in the Winter Hill mining enterprises.

On most Ordnance Survey maps - even the very latest edition of the Explorer West Pennine Moor chart - the Winter Hill Tunnel (SD 66329 14676) is marked just to the north west of the TV mast on the left hand side of the footpath running down to Belmont Road. All through my life I have wondered where this tunnel went to, but have never ever managed to find anyone who knew any details about it. The location of it is easy to spot and there were obviously two entrances next to each other. There is also a fairly obvious track leading from the mine to the present footpath so it is safe to assume that coal extracted from this entrance was taken down to Belmont rather than being hauled across to moor to Horwich.

Due to the recent discovery of an old mining map (or to be more honest a dawning realisation of the location of coal mines on a map I'd had for years) I can now tell all those folk who have long wondered about the Winter Hill Tunnel exactly where it goes. The tunnel is fairly straight and runs in a southerly direction for a distance of 300 yards passing through areas of coal which were removed by "William Garbutt and William Ailam Mason" probably around the 1850's. The end of this straight tunnel lies approximately directly opposite the main entrance to the TV station underneath the suspension cables. At the end of the tunnel is a maze of old workings with another major roadway heading southwards towards the Number 7 and 8 shafts which were about 700 yards from the Winter Hill Tunnel entrance near to the road up the hill to the TV mast. The number 7 & 8 shafts appear on both the Mountain Mine plan and that of the Winter Hill Tunnel.

If you walk down the footpath about 100 yards lies the remains of the "New Tunnel" entrance to the coal workings on the right hand side of the path. The location can be easily spotted due to the spoil heaps – and the millstone grit sidewall of the entrance can be easily found. Judging from the state of the surface above the line of the tunnel heading up the hill, it is safe to assume that that it has all collapsed since the mine was closed.

The ground surrounding the Winter Hill Tunnel entrances also shows signs of extensive underground collapses near to the entrance.

++

Heather matters: *redressing the balance*

Clive Weake & Ian Harper

The West Pennine Moors, which cover ninety square miles of moorlands, valleys, farmland and reservoirs in south Lancashire, have seen a 50% loss in heather cover, mostly between 1963 and 1988. Clive Weake and Ian Harper describe the projects taking place to redress the balance.

The attraction of the landscape and all that it holds has made the moors a traditional recreational venue for many generations of local people from the surrounding towns of Bury and Bolton in the south and Accrington, Blackburn, Chorley and Preston to the north and west.

As this pressure has increased, management of the area has been co-ordinated through the West Pennine Moors Recreation and Conservation Plan. The work of the plan is taken forward by Lancashire County Council with support and funding from North West Water, Bury and Bolton Metropolitan Borough Councils and the Countryside Commission.

The management takes many forms including the provision of recreational facilities, access, information and interpretation, working with local communities, and also conserving wildlife and landscape. West Pennines has large open expanses of moorland, nearly all of which is used for rough grazing. Up to the late 1950s and early 1960s much of the moorland had a good cover of heather and bilberry, but since the disappearance of the gamekeepers who were employed by the previous Liverpool and Bolton Water Corporations, the moors have suffered from grazing and large uncontrolled fires. As a result, much of the moorland is now dominated by *Molinia*.

A recent survey commissioned by the West Pennine Moors Conservation Advisory Committee used three sets of aerial photographs dated 1946, 1963 and 1988 to chart the rate of decline of heather cover. Figures showing the amount lost and the rate of decline were most disturbing, revealing a 50% loss in heather cover mostly between 1963 and 1988.

The Countryside Rangers have now started the daunting task of redressing the balance. The first project converted 4 ha of rough grazing on Anglezarke Moor just north of Belmont Village and part of Manor House Farm.

The second project will take in 15 ha of rough grazing at Higher Pasture House Farm to the east of Belmont, using funding from the Countryside Stewardship Scheme.

The following procedure was used on the 4 ha project following advice from John Phillips of the Joseph Nickerson Reconciliation Trust, whose staff have pioneered this work in Scotland:

March 1991. The previous winter's build-up of dead grass was burnt off. At the same time strips were burnt into existing heather stands on the north west slopes of Anglezarke Moor, to prepare for heather seed collection.
August 1991. The area was left until the resulting fresh growth of grass was flowering. Roundup herbicide was then applied to kill off the grass.
September 1991. The grass had completely died back, six weeks after the application. The area was then burnt again to get rid of the dead material.
November 1991. The remaining tussocks and top two inches of peat/soil were rotavated.
December 1991. The area was fenced out from the rest of the moor to protect the plot from sheep grazing.
The seed trash collected from Anglezarke Moor using a vacuum technique was applied. These seeds germinated and appeared as seedlings in July 1992. These are now very healthy plants.

February 1992. Some of the area was covered with trash from heather bales donated by the North York Moors National Park. Germination has taken longer but there is now a high density of young seedlings.

May 1992. More seed trash was collected from the burnt strips and put down in July 1992. These have now germinated and the young seedlings are easily seen. The remaining areas of the plot were seeded in April and July 1993 and should germinate in 1994.

Heather seed

Seed has been collected from the Moores Estate adjacent to Wycoller Country Park using a vacuum technique, and seed collected from North West Water's Longdendale Estate in the Peak District, using a harvester made available by the Joseph Nickerson Reconciliation Trust.

The heather seed trash was applied at a rate of 10 grams/square metre, i.e. less than a handful. We have estimated that there are approximately 320 seeds/10 grams and it is expected that 65% will germinate.

Now that seeds have germinated successfully, future trash will be mixed with sawdust in order to spread it further. Up until now the seed has been broadcast by hand. On the larger scheme it is intended to use mechanical seedling with a standard tractor-mounted spreader.

Herbicide

Roundup was applied at a rate of 6 litres/ha. A high concentration is required to kill off the *Molinia*. This herbicide has been approved as safe to use in catchment areas by North West Water.

Regrowth

Disturbance of the peat by rotavating has resulted in a fresh growth of rushes and rose-bay willow-herb. The rushes have been spot treated with Roundup, while the willow-herb has been handpulled. The grasses are now beginning to grow back. This does not present a problem as the heather seedlings are now established and should be able to compete.

Grazing

It is hoped that light summer grazing will be introduced in 1995 or 1996 to keep grasses down and encourage the heather to till out. The fence is unlikely to be removed as the plot will offer good grazing on the edge of a large unproductive moorland, so the sheep would over-concentrate on it.

Future work
The present plot is a very small proportion of Anglezarke Moor (0.3%). We would like to continue and extend the work but this is dependent on the farmer agreeing to give up more land. Constraints will be long fence lines and finding sufficient heather seed.
One option would be to restore large areas without fencing thus reducing the impact of grazing damage. The scheme is intended to start the ball rolling and encourage others to take on the initiative or at least become more involved.

Monitoring
Monitoring of progress on the first plot will start this November using quadrats and fixed point photography. We are discussing a system for monitoring both the extension of the work on to the wider area of moorland and the effect of changing sheep grazing regimes.
This will involve Lancashire County Council Planning Department. It is quite possible that changes in grazing will have positive effects and lead to overall improvement in heather cover.

Problems
The biggest difficulty with the project has been establishing a reliable source of heather seed, which is not commercially available at a realistic price:
- It is not possible to keep collecting from Anglezarke Moor as there are few heather stands suitable for strip burning.
- The heather bales from North Yorks Moors National Park were of great value, but this is not a realistic source for the much bigger schemes we are now working on, for which a larger number of bales would have to be transported.
- The seed from the Moores Estate, Wycoller, was collected by contractor using a vacuum technique. We will continue to pursue this as a supply, but there are constraints of time and weather.

- The seed from Longdendale is a good source and we are currently looking into the possibilities of ensuring a regular supply of large quantities of seed.

Where we go from here on the large scale is a complex issue involving the tenant farmer, the landowner North West Water and possible shooting interests. To carry out large scale works would require a major cash input which means that the farmer and landowner would be looking for a return.

The conservation budgets available through West Pennines are limited and intended to prime projects.

Clive Weake was Head Countryside Ranger, West Pennine Moors.
Ian Harper was Access Area Countryside Ranger, West Pennine Moors.

++

The Whimberry Hill Area.

This is an area of Winter Hill which is much ignored by most people and on many days it is possible to walk all over the moorland from Scout Road to Belmont, without even **seeing** a living soul let alone meeting one - even in summer. Although superficially it appears totally bleak and desolate with nothing of any real interest, for the searcher, there is much to be seen and many mysteries to be explained.

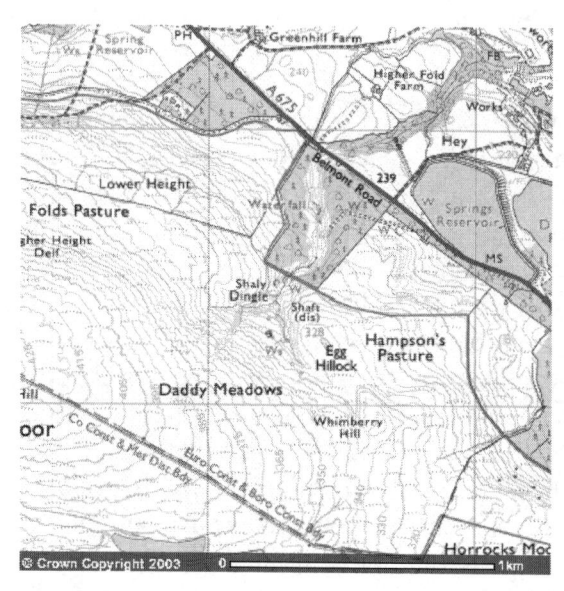

Perhaps one of the reasons for the lack of visitors, is the fact that there is no really easy access point to the area despite the main Belmont Road passing nearby. The nearest access points are either from the quarries on Scout Road or the path starting opposite the Wright Arms at Belmont.

On the Ordnance Survey maps, no footpaths are shown in this area except for the Wilton Arms to the TV mast footpath – but footpaths DO exist -although in places they get a bit "thin" and indistinct. Off the paths the going can be a little rough as much is that awful "hillock" grass which is just perfect for twisting ankles - and in summer some parts are covered in bracken. There are patches of heather all over the place. The one form of vegetation which does NOT exist on or near Whimberry Hill, is whimberries! This is perhaps indicative of how, over a period of time, the whole character of an area can change. There is just no way that a hill can be named Whimberry Hill if they didn't actually grow there in earlier centuries. The area is bordered by Scout Road to the East, Belmont Road to the North, Dean Ditch to the South and the Wright Arms footpath to the West. The area contains numerous quarries, a large number of wells, some peculiar underground watercourses, geologically interesting small valleys, an old coal mine, a wood (private property with no access) which is full of pheasants/grouse and much more of interest.

We'll start with the quarries. By far the biggest ones are Horrocks Fold Quarries on either side of Scout Road but on the moorland there are many others to be seen …. Spakes Delph, Martha Tree Dell, Sandstone Delph, and Higher Height Delph, Coal Road Delfs ……..all are – or were, the main ones. All produced sandstone/millstone grit. There is no evidence of any form of drilling in the early quarries so the rocks were probably removed with wedges and other implements.

To the Western side of the spur forming Whimberry Hill is a small valley which contains some rather odd things connected with water. Firstly there is a "well or shaft" …. illustrated above. This is near the termination of the northern end of one of the great ditches running from the top of Winter Hill.

On the 1849 Ordnance Survey maps it is marked as a shaft. The shaft is only a few feet deep and is filled with rubble. Right next to this, is an underground watercourse, a tunnel about 2 feet in height with stone walls and stone slabs forming the roof with soil and vegetation on top. Parts of this tunnel have collapsed and the structure can be clearly seen.

The culvert was obviously dug out and roofed ….. but for what reason? The place forms a natural valley anyway and a stream would have flowed down it quite naturally. Why was it covered? More to the point, where does it start and finish? Is there a connection between the shaft and the watercourse for the two are right next to each other. At various places along the course of the tunnel, the roof has collapsed but I have still not been able to trace either its exact course or it's start and finish point. Perhaps others may be luckier!

On the Ordnance Survey map of 1849 the wells and tunnels are shown, but again there is no hint to the exact purpose of them. On the map, the course of the tunnel (or rather tunnels as there are apparently two of them although I've only managed to find one) is shown with the word "Well" at the "entrance" of it. All rather odd!

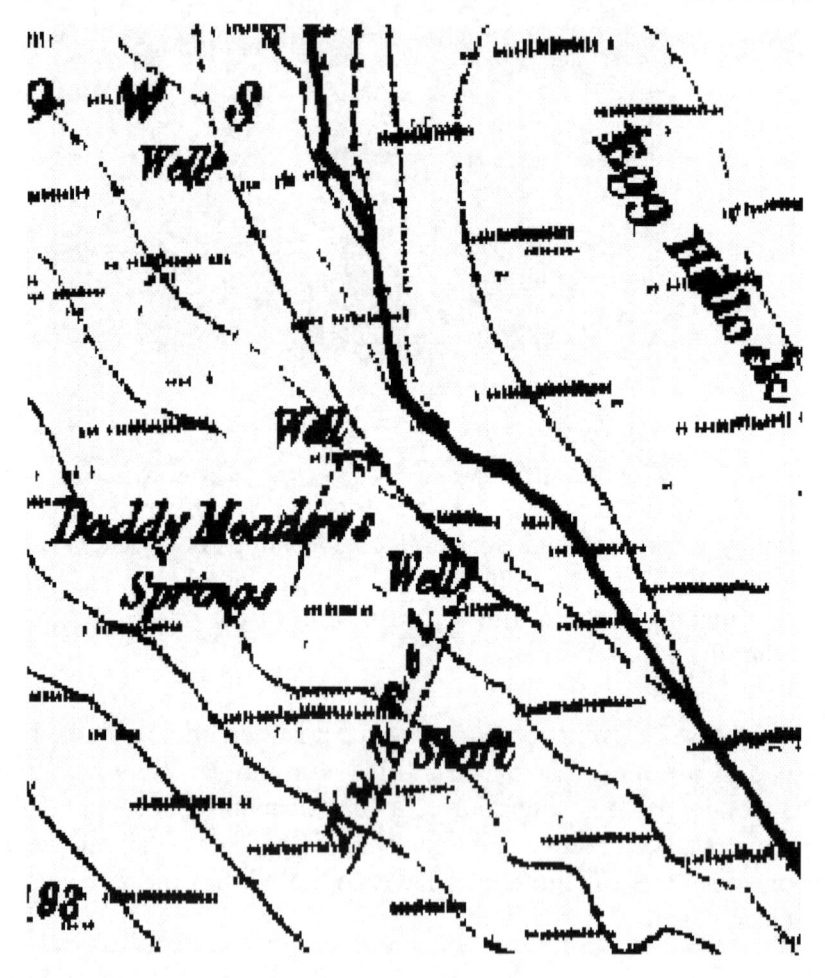

Moving Westwards we come to Shaly Dingle, an apt name for the place as various streams in the locality have cut through the surface boulder clay down to the bed rock exposing layers of shale on the sides. The beds of many of the streams are covered with pieces of this shale (some contain fossils).

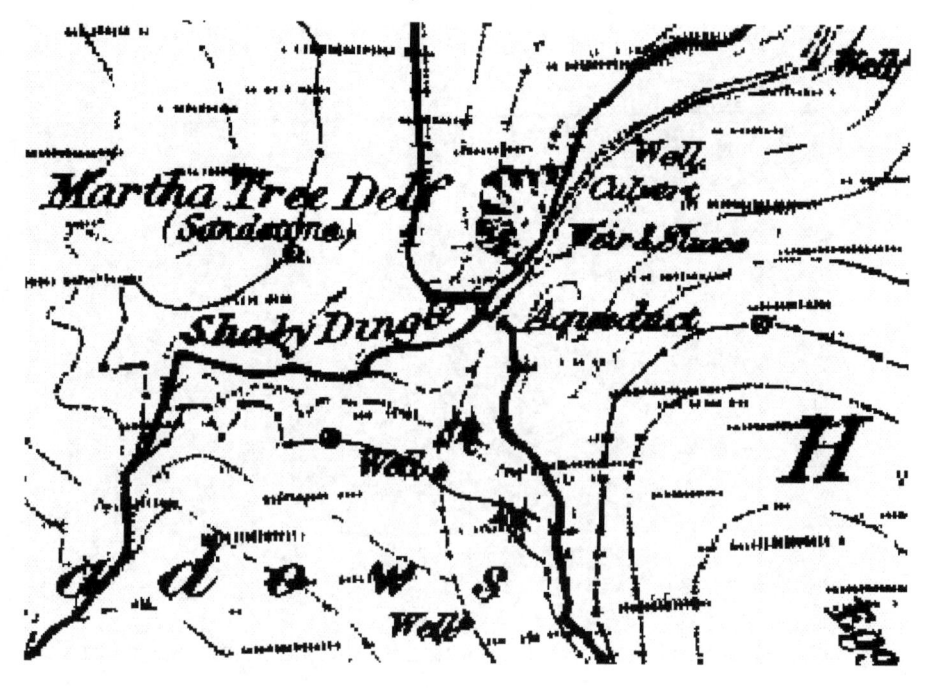

On the modern day maps there is little marked on the chart but on earlier maps.

Shaly Dingle lies at the confluence of three streams, the water being channelled into Springs Reservoir which lies on the other side of Belmont Road. In this small area, there are wells, an old coal mine and a quarry.

The coal mine can be seen in the south eastern tributary on the western bank, and it appears to be a standard NCB concrete capped shaft complete with the odd tapering square block on top. I can find no record of any details of this mine. Centuries ago people must have been aware of the coal in the area as the odd coal seam can be clearly seen in the banks of some streams nearby – complete with coniferous fossils.

On the hill in between the south eastern and south western tributaries lie a number of walled shafts. On old maps four of these are marked as "wells". They all lie fairly near to springs where the water comes out of the ground. At present I can find no information about these wells or their purpose ….. were they for nearby homes, or perhaps for the local mine or were they connected in some way with the nearby reservoirs?

The wells are all fairly shallow, a deeper one is covered with a wire grill and all are filled with stone rubble, some have a small amount of water at the bottom and most are beautifully decorated in moss and ferns. Well worth a look! In summer the grass and bracken surrounding them will be much higher and it may be difficult to find some of them at that season.

Each of the tributaries are worth investigation if only for the geology visible in some of them. The northern heading tributary is perhaps the most interesting. The stream has cut through the boulder clay and near the surface it contains a large number of rounded stones formed by glacial action many years ago. Lower down, the stream has cut through the gritstone rock which is greatly faulted and the current bed of the stream is formed of the carboniferous period shales. Several coal seams are visible in the sides of the stream along with the associated fireclays. Leaf and tree fossils can be found near the coal seams.

At one point I found in the bed of the stream, a block of sandstone clearly showing the ripple marks caused by the tides when this rock was sand lying on the bottom of a shallow sea. The rock showed various layers of ripples as each successive tide put down another layer of sand and then rippled that new layer as well. All this happened "on Winter Hill". Amazing!

Also visible in the walls and beds of the streams are small rocks whose composition clearly illustrates the moving power of early glacial action in the area, lumps of granite probably carried southwards from Cumbria or Scotland along with quartzite rocks from who knows where. Go take a look!

There is a fairly large and active spring in the eastern bank of the main stream (the middle one!) but all over the place are bits of fairly modern clay piping indicating that that perhaps in Victorian times attempts were made to "pipe" this water to some other place. Anyone got any ideas or information about this?

Just below the confluence of the three tributaries is an interesting display of brickwork. At one point, the pathway crosses over the south eastern stream with a brick embankment, the stream passing underneath through an attractive arched hole. On old maps this is marked as "aqueduct" so one assumes pipes or something similar – surely not an open waterway – passed over this structure. Lower downstream is a large brick embankment on the eastern side of the stream marked on the map as "weir and sluice" although I see no signs today of any weir or sluice!
On the opposite bank is the Martha Tree Delph Sandstone Quarry along with a rusted piece of rail, presumably used for tubbing the

stone out of the quarry. A pipe with flowing water sticks out into the stream from underneath the quarry but there is no clue as to where this water originates. Perhaps the quarry was considerably deeper than it is today (it was in use in the early 1800's and perhaps even earlier) and the water is coming from the original floor of the quarry.

Downstream, the stream enters the private plantation of conifers but over the fence yet another well can be seen by the side of the track.

This woodland is one of the beauty spots of the whole area, and it is a great pity that it is closed to the public. In the middle of the wood is a magnificent waterfall in a majestic setting especially when the

stream is in full flow following heavy rain. Within the woodland there is an old tunnel that has been explored for a distance of about 150 feet - but it is almost completely silted up at that point and further progress is impossible. It is not known whether the tunnel was dug for coal or water purposes – there is however no sign of coal and as the tunnel heads in the general direction of further wells, it is assumed that the tunnel was at one time connected to the water supplies of the area.

The foundations of the TV mast.

(*This article appeared in "The Structural Engineer" January 1966 No 1 Vol 44*)

The anchor blocks are constructed of mass concrete to resist the uplift component from the stays and are normally designed with a safety factor of two. The blocks are also checked for passive pressure on the front face to resist horizontal movement. The mast base of a conventional pinned structure is designed to support the direct thrust and the shear.

The base for each of the 1265 ft masts consisted of a large reinforced concrete raft to carry the six columns of the superstructure. These rafts were 35 ft square and 5 ft 6 in thick. However, due to the presence of old mine workings under Winter Hill, an extensive soil investigation was necessary. A search through the records of the National Coal Board showed that these mines had been worked between 1861 and 1881 but the extent and size was not at all clear from the available maps.

One borehole was taken at the mast base to a depth of 120 ft and one at each of the outer anchor block positions down to 50 ft. Seismic soundings were also taken but owing to a heavy overlay of peat these were not considered reliable.

The boreholes showed the workings to occur between 44 and 47 feet below the ground. Although it was difficult to predict the degree of settlement, it was likely that differential movement would occur and this could not be tolerated with a fixed base design. In the circumstances it was decided to sink four 6 ft 6 in diameter shafts, one in each corner of the 28 ft square base.

The shafts were lined with precast tunnel sections for their full depth, the sections being added to the bottom as the work progressed. When nearing the mine workings special precautions had to be taken in case either gas or water was encountered with the breakthrough. Fortunately, however, neither was encountered. When all four shafts had been sunk, the workings in the immediate vicinity of the mast base were compacted with a mixture of sand and weak concrete. The columns were constructed so they were free standing within the shafts to allow for a limited horizontal movement of the ground. The columns were founded about 5 ft below the workings on good quality rock (see diagram).

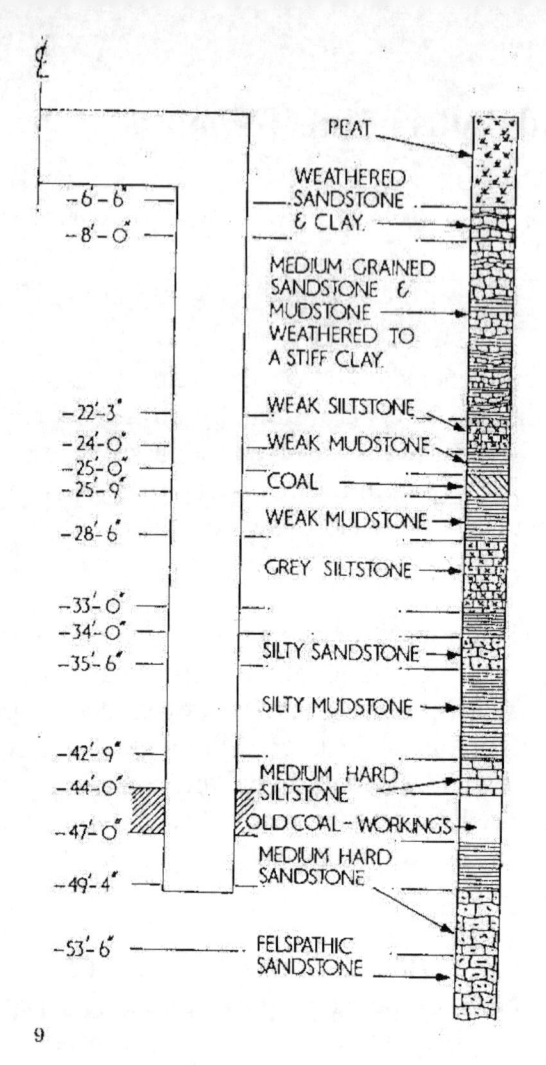

The anchor blocks were basically of traditional design, except that to provide the necessary passive resistance the fronts of the blocks were were extended down into the solid ground below the peat. This resulted in a variation in block design depending on the depth of peat at each location. At one or two positions small streams ran a few feet in front of the blocks and it was necessary to divert these as an additional precaution.

Earthing of masts is not normally a difficult problem. The structure is earthed at its base by means of aluminium or copper tape connected to earth plates or rods sunk into the ground. The stays are also earthed in a similar manner

TV Mast Construction Photo's
(Thanks to Bill Learmouth for the photo's)

WINTER HILL TV COVERAGE AREA. (Analogue TV only)

BBC 1 (North West)   ch 55
BBC 2   ch 62
ITV   ch 59
Channel 4   ch 65
Power (Max erp, vision)   100 kW
Polarisation   horizontal
Receiving aerial group   C/D
Mean ht. of aerial   294m agl, 732m aod
Transmitter site   near Horwich, Gtr. Manchester
National Grid Reference   SD 660144

Key: Service area
     : Relay station ▲

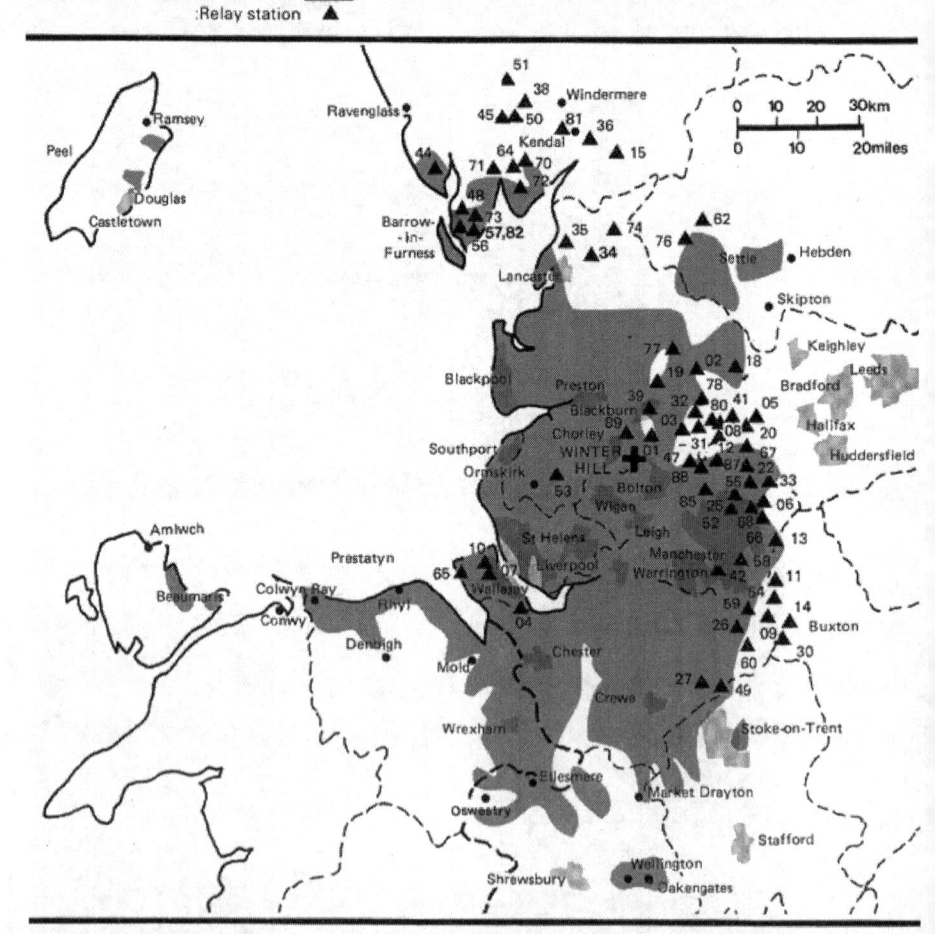

The service area is indicated by the coloured part of the map, but the boundary should not be interpreted as a rigid limit. As the quality of television reception can be very different at places only short distances apart, there are, inevitably, small pockets of poor reception which cannot be shown.
Details of relay stations are shown overleaf in numerical order.

The Making of the Mast ….. by William Kay of Adlington …… *by William Kay*

The television station on Winter Hill in Lancashire was built for the Independent Television Authority, (later the Independent Broadcasting Authority), which had been set up by Parliament to broadcast and control the Commercial TV services then coming into being

The Winter Hill station was built during 1956 and '57 and broadcasting of Granada programmes commenced in Sept 1957, the transmitting aerials for the service being mounted at the top of a 450ft steel tower which resembled a large electricity pylon. The services at that time were in the 405 line VHS system, but with the proposed introduction of 625 line UHF system and a requirement that BBC1 & 2 should also transmit from Winter Hill, it became obvious that the 450 ft tower would be inadequate for the job. The ITA therefore decided to erect a new mast and to this end commissioned a 1000 ft one of novel design from British Insulated Callender Construction (BICC).

This mast was to be of cylindrical construction and to be held up by stay lines (thick guy wires). Work commenced on the new structure in 1964 with the digging of an enormous hole for the foundations, which were to consist of a large concrete raft with four corner legs, rather like a table. Interestingly, three of the four shafts, dug to accommodate these legs unexpectedly intercepted old coal mine shafts which had to be backfilled and strengthened before the foundations could be started. In the centre on top of the raft was built a reinforced concrete base to which the tubular mast was to be bolted. This was a break with the convention as guyed masts are usually supported on a single large ball bearing to accommodate all the swaying and twisting movements that occur in these structures.

The tubular mast body was then erected by the process of bolting half cylindrical sections of galvanised steel each 10 ft high and 9 ft diameter to each other, work thus progressing at the rate of 10 ft per 2 lifts of steel. The early lifts were accomplished by the use of a transportable crane. At this stage an ingenious device was brought into play consisting of a long steel tube with a jib crane head fixed to its end. This was mounted vertically inside the mast cylinder and used to lift the sections. As these were added, the jib crane was jacked up and relocated into the next section, and so was always in position for the next lift.

As the mast grew, temporary stay lines were attached to it to steady it until eventually the anchor points for the permanent stays were installed and those final stays fitted. The construction of the mast was completed in 1965. As much of the work took place in the depth of winter, one must admire the courage, fitness and tenacity of the rigging staff who carried out this work in often freeing conditions At this point it should be noted that the mast isn't quite what it seems, in fact the 9 ft steel cylinder only goes to 600 ft after which it changes into a lattice mast for the rest of its height. The transmission aerials for all the TV services are mounted in this section However this section is itself covered by a cylinder of about 11 ft diameter, this being made of fibreglass, which acts as a weather shield whilst allowing the transmission waves to pass through. The overall height of the mast is 1015 ft. For ease of access to aerials a passenger lift going to 600 ft was installed during the original construction.

Two further masts of this type were built, both 1250ft tall at Emley Moor near Huddersfield, and the other one in Lincolnshire, giving ITV and BBC services to those regions. Then, Horror of Horrors, in March 1969, in the face of severe icing up and adverse weather conditions, the Emley Moor mast collapsed. Anxious eyes, (particularly my own, as I was on duty under the Winter Hill one at that time), were directed to the Winter Hill mast and its remaining sister in Lincolnshire, both of which were heavily iced up. Luckily they survived, but both of them were subjected to intense investigation and to a programme of modification and strengthening over the past ten years. Now it is probably true to say that they are as safe as any mast in Europe.

Over in Yorkshire, where the TV service was restored within four days, using temporary structures, the fallen mast had damaged some property and closed a road The Local District Council were reluctant to allow erection of another permanent mast, but eventually a compromise was reached and the present concrete tower was built to carry the broadcast services The above events make it unlikely that any further cylindrical masts of the Winter Hill type and height will ever be erected. Also, as terrestrial Digital TV and Satellite services progress, the need for these structure will recede. Footnote: When the 1000 ft mast came into operation, the original 450 ft tower at Winter Hill was dismantled and rebuilt in Scotland where it continues to give sterling service.

The Night the Welsh invaded Winter Hill! ….. *by William Kay*

It was 21.05 hours on a typical Winter Hill early March evening (the 4 March 1977 to be exact) when the assault was made. The night was clear and stars were shining, however a thin ground mist wreathed the road and moor land. I was the senior shift engineer on duty that night along with two other shift engineers, Mike Ingram and Peter Dennis.

Peter was manning the control desk, whilst I was in the test room repairing some piece of equipment. By a stroke of good fortune Mike was just heading for the kitchen via the entrance hail when the incident began. He rushed to the test room and informed me that we had intruders on the premises. I immediately followed him to the hall where I saw that the glass panel in the front door had been broken to gain access and I was just in time to see someone going away from me down the corridor leading via the garage to the UHF transmitter hall. I shouted to Peter to contact the Police and then, accompanied by Mike, followed the intruders into the UHF transmitter hall I switched on the lights as I went for the intruders were using torches.

On entering the transmitter hall I saw four people, two young men and two young women in the room. One of the women was operating the HT Isolator and earthing switches of the 'A' transmitter, (almost the quickest way of switching off).
I immediately challenged her but she continued to operate the switches. I went up to the transmitter and switched it back on again. In all there was a break in transmission of about 15 seconds. I subsequently found out the 'B' transmitter had also been switched of by the same method. The intruders made no effort to stop me re-powering the transmitters; they just stood back from me whilst I did it. As I stood there guarding the 'A' transmitter whilst Mike stood by

the 'B' I noticed that one of the women was carrying a carpenter's hammer. I was glad I hadn't spotted that before.

When my panic subsided and I was in control of myself and of the situation, I questioned them about their motives They informed me they were members of the Welsh Language Society and that the intended disruption of the Winter Hill transmissions was part of their campaign for a 4th channel for Welsh speaking Wales. Winter Hill had been chosen because Granada programmes beamed from it not only covered NW England but also leaked over into north Wales, and this they objected to. I tried to explain that radio and tv signals are no respecters of geographical or political boundaries, and I tried to point out to them that inhabitants of N. Wales did not have to tune their sets to the Granada channel if they did not wish to receive it. But all this fell on deaf ears.

At about 20.25 hrs the Police arrived, first the Horwich police, then those from Chorley and lastly the PC from Adlngton. As the Winter Hill station is actually on the Chorley side of the boundary, and in the Adlington section of the Chorley Police area, then the privilege or pain of arresting the culprits fell to the Adlington PC.

When the prisoners were searched, there was found in the handbag of one of the women, a quantity of 6in nails. The idea had been to disrupt the transmission and then to barricade themselves in the transmitter hall by nailing all the doors shut, thus preventing early re-powering of the transmitters. This part of the plan luckily was thwarted by our good luck and Mike's prompt actions. This was of course the reason the woman was carrying the hammer. The Police questioned me closely as to whether at any time they had threatened us with the hammer, but in all truth, I had to say that the group behaved impeccably after being challenged. In fact it seemed a major part of their policy was to get arrested and go to court to extract the maximum publicity for their cause.

As the Police were leaving they asked what would be the cost of replacing the glass door. Just off the top of my head I said '£100'. It was eventually replaced at a cost of £30 but the damages set by the court and paid by the miscreants was the sum of £100, so that night I made a profit of £70 for the IBA. The group pleaded guilty and were sentenced to some months in prison I believe.

The Welsh finally got their 4th channel but when 1 look at the programmes that appear on all channels in general, I often wonder if those four people still think it was worth their sacrifice.

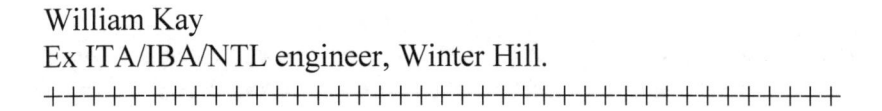

William Kay
Ex ITA/IBA/NTL engineer, Winter Hill.
++

Horwich Water supplies from Montcliffe Colliery.

In the late 1800's, the rapidly expanding town of Horwich was desperately short of water. Despite being surrounded by water catchment areas and reservoirs, the town itself had great difficulty in providing clean water for its inhabitants as all the water supplies in the area were owned by other towns and cities. Things reached crisis point in the 1880's and something had to be done about the water shortage.

The following paper is taken from the memoirs of the Manchester Geological Society of 1891 which explains both the problem and the solution.

Water Supply at Horwich

By Mr Joseph Crankshaw.

A glance at the map of Horwich and district shows the surface of the ground studded over with reservoirs, some of them an extent as to be denominated lakes. On the North, the Belmont watershed is appropriated by the Bolton Corporation Waterworks, a series of bleachworks extending right away down to Bolton. On the East are the large reservoirs of the Halliwell Bleachworks, and Dean Mills. To the South-east the Bolton Corporation have been tunnelling for years in the Millstone Grit, and are now constructing a large reservoir for storage of the water found. On the West the Liverpool

Waterworks appropriates the upland waters from Rivington Moor and a large share of Wildersmoor. In the township itself the staple industry, up to quite recently, was bleaching, for which a large quantity of good water is required. In 1876 the Blackrod Local Board obtained power to construct a reservoir which impounds a portion of the surface water from Wildersmoor, and also springs in Wilderswood and underground waters from old coal workings.

It will thus be seen that the district Is one in which there is plenty of water, and the water, whether in streams from the breezy uplands, or in springs which gush forth from the millstone grit, is of good quality.

Up to 1884 there was no town water supply. The place was sparsely populated, and each group of cottages had its spring or well, and although there were dry seasons when the wells and springs dried up, and the inhabitants had to carry water from considerable distances, still they never suffered anything like the same inconveniences from scarcity of water as other districts, or even as the neighbouring townships of Blackrod and Aspull. After the public spirit shown by Blackrod in constructing their large reservoir in Horwich, and appropriating the best available supply, the Horwich Local Board seemed to think that something should be done, and a considerable sum of money was dribbled away, in making half-hearted enquiries into various schemes which were afterwards abandoned, and ultimately an arrangement was made with the Blackrod Local Board for 50,000 gallons of water per day at 6d per 1,000 gallons. In 1885, the Lancashire and Yorkshire Railway Company decided to bring their Locomotive works to Horwich, and the place, after being at a standstill for years at once became a busy scene of activity, building being carried on in all directions, and a largely increased water supply being required. The dry season of 1887 completely exhausted the Blackrod storage, and the Horwich Local Board were informed that they would have to look elsewhere for their requirements for over 50,000 gallons per day. Under the circumstances the Blackrod supply could never be anything but partial, as the level of the reservoir was far too low to supply the higher parts of Horwich.

The Horwich Local Board found that they had allowed the whole of their watershed to be appropriated, and the only water supply available was from the Moncliffe Colliery belonging to Messrs H Mason & Son. Popular prejudice was very much against this water, as it was imagined that because it was pumped at a colliery it must of necessity be contaminated, but this had to some extent been overcome by the dry season, when temporary arrangements were made for pumping the water into the Blackrod reservoir, where it constituted practically the whole water supply.

The Local Board also found that it was a case of Hobson's Choice, one or none, this being the only feasible scheme available, so Messres Frank France and James Atherton, of Bolton, were authorised to inquire into this supply, and the following extract from their report fully explains the scheme, and may be of some interest to the members of this society :-

"In reporting on the question of the obtaining of a water supply for your Board's District from the shaft at Montcliffe, in addition to the 50,000 gallons per day now obtained from the Blackrod Local Board, we think it may be desirable to state, first the conditions under which the water is found, then to remark on its quality, the freedom from pollution or otherwise of its surroundings, and the mode in which it may be made to serve all the populated parts of the district.

Firstly, as to the conditions under which it is found:-

The water is found near to the bottom of a shaft which was sunk many years ago at Montcliffe, in the higher part of Horwich, for the purpose of winning a mine of coal and fireclay. The shaft is 130 yards deep, and is sunk through strata which consists mostly of sandstone and shale, the geological formation being that known as "Millstone Grit". No water appears in the mine on the higher side of the shaft, nor along the level proceeding from the bottom of the shaft, but at the inspection recently made by us we found the water made in some straight roadways which had been driven on the deep of the shaft, and only a short distance away therefrom. In these roadways the water poured in continuous streams from the roof, and as it had passed through beds of sandstone of so great a thickness, it seemed evident that it must be well filtered. In appearance the water was bright and clear, and the floor on which it continually gathered showed that it contained the merest trace of iron. This is not often the case in water associated with coal mines.

On arriving at the water we took a sample for analysis. A second sample was taken near the pump foot, to reach which it was necessary to walk partly through the water necessitating a slight disturbance. A third sample was taken on the surface at a point known as the "Tunnel Mouth" hereafter referred to. The three samples were sealed up on the spot and were afterwards forwarded to Dr Frankland, of London, for analysis, in order to ascertain the fitness of the water for domestic use.

We made a careful inspection underground with a view to ascertain if the water was likely in any way to be fouled by the workings of the colliery.

We found all the coal lying on the easterly side of a 26 yards fault, hereafter referred to, had been won with the exception of pillars left to support the roadway between the pumping and ventilating shafts, and a small area now being worked some 150 yards on the rise of the first-named shaft.

Throughout these workings the strata were entirely dry, and as a consequence not a drop of water finds its way from the parts where the workmen travel to the water which is the subject of this report. The present surroundings of the water may be considered absolutely free from, and liability to, polluting influences. This being so, we made inquiry if it was likely these conditions would remain.

The mine has been worked out to the beforementioned fault, which runs in a direction SW to NE, and at a distance of about 200 yards on the W side of the pumping shaft. And about 170 yards to the west of it, and the coal still remaining to be got under the present lease lies to the north and west of this fault, throwing the mine down 26 yards. To win this coal (which has not hitherto been worked) the ventilating shaft (which is 170 yards on the west or rise of the pumping shaft) will have to be sunk 26 yards, and the coal raised there, instead of (as at present) at the pumping shaft. In this case this shaft would only be used for pumping. This would be a further guarantee against the possibility of pollution of the water. Whether any water might be found in the new workings, could only be ascertained by proving, and if there was, it would be at a lower level.

The hamlet of Montcliffe can be seen at the top centre of the picture. The water from the mine travelled along a pipe from the pumping shaft, this being located in a tunnel which emerged just to the north of the reservoir. The reservoir is now no longer used and is dry (not surprising as there is a huge gap in one of the retaining walls!)

We found the pumping shaft in very good condition, and the rams and pump stocks which were in the shaft in perfect order. The pumping engine is of a very good make (Messrs Hathorn, Davies and Co, Sun Foundary, Leeds) and of recent construction. To raise all the water made at present requires only 4.5 to 5 strokes per minute, equal to about 140,000 gallons per day of 24 hours, besides which 9,000 gallons are pumped to the surface for the supply of the houses at Montcliffe. This we consider (after the exceptionally long drought of the past summer) may be taken as the minimum yield. In winter the engine is said to run at about 6 strokes per minute, if it was run at 10 strokes 358,000 gallons would be delivered in the 24 hours. The pumps are in duplicate, there being two rams each of 10 inch diameter, and two sets of pump stocks. These are arranged so that either set can be worked in case of accident. The pumping arrangements are very good.

Quality of the water.

The result of Dr Franklands analysis is:- The water is excellent in quality for drinking and all dietic purposes". He states also – "that it contains the merest trace of organic matter" and "is entirely free from any evidence of contamination with sewage or other animal refuse matters".

These analyses prove the water to be of a very superior character for domestic purposes.

++

Winter Hill Summit and Dean Ditch Area.

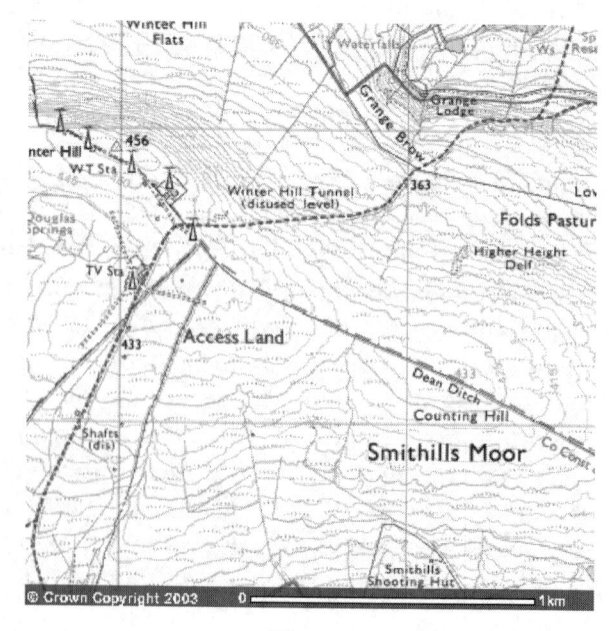

This area of Winter Hill is a mixture of the ancient and modern, from the remains of bygone times to the technology of the future. The future is represented by the plethora of radio and TV masts which are scattered near the peak and have slowly grown in number over the last few decades.

The first mast to be built was the large one located to the east of the OS survey column that was erected in 1948 initially for police communications. It now houses a lot more than antennas for the police! The next mast to be built was the original IBA TV mast which arrived in 1955 but this was soon replaced by the present structure which is over 1,000 feet high (328 metres). The Post Office mast was built in 1955.

The exact figures I have for the height is that it is 1,015 feet 4 in tall and the transmitters have a range of round about 50 miles covering the Manchester and Liverpool conurbation's and within it's area it reaches over 7 million people. It's known as an "enclosed cylindrical mast" and it used to have a lift inside it – but now the engineers and riggers have to climb up a vertical ladder – or rig up a cradle to one of the cables on the outside. They have to climb up to maintain the aerials, paint the mast and to ensure that the red aircraft lights are working.

The transmitters do not have to be switched off for routine maintenance as all the systems are doubled up so the mast can continue broadcasting if something fails. If there is a really serious fault it can be run on reduced power until the engineers can sort out the problem. The station is run using only skeleton staff and is remotely controlled from another location.

All the masts at the top of the hill are used for a variety of communications purposes for local services, businesses and organisations.

The TV channels transmitting via the TV mast are BBC1, BBC2, ITV (Granada), Channel 4 and Channel 5 aong with the new Freeview digital channels. Radio channels transmitted from here include Radio's 1, 2, 3 and 4 along with Rock FM, Jazz FM, Century 105 and BBC Radio Lancashire.

In the early days when the original TV mast was built, it was thought that there may have been a risk to the resident engineers in times of inclement weather. In view of this a building was erected part way down the moorland road where the staff used to be housed at those times. The wooden structure was removed many years ago but the metal fence that used to house it, still remains. The mast still presents dangers for the unwary in the winter months, when icicles can form on the support cables which crash to the ground if a sudden thaw occurs. You have been warned!

Dean Ditch.

From the mast heading eastwards towards Horrocks Moor and Scout Road is the seemingly endless drystone wall which was built to mark the municipal boundaries. On modern maps this is marked as the County Constitutional and Metropolitan District/European Constitutional and Borough boundary. The wall is quite a feat of engineering and must have taken some considerable time to build. It seems to vary in height between six and seven feet for its whole length of almost 3 kilometres. There are few quaries near the hill top and although rocks can be found on the surface the bulk of the material to make the wall must have been carried up the hill. I have not spotted any gates or breaks in the original wall although parts of it are now in a fairly poor state.

The dry-stone wall follows the route of an ancient ditch which although today is known as Dean ditch, it was originally called Dane or Danes Ditch. A number of place names in this area indicate that the Danes once settled in this part of Lancashire (and don't forget the Scandinavian stone axe found in Tigers Clough dating from before 2,000BC) and from pollen analysis we know that much of the deforestation of the moor took place around this period so perhaps the name Danes Ditch may not be too wide of the mark. The ditch is not visible for the full length of the wall but even when it vanishes, its route can be traced through the slightly differing colour of the vegetation seen at certain times of the year.

A footpath runs along the full length of the wall and the panoramic views available on clear days makes this a good place to stretch the legs. The path starts at the stile at the side of the most south easterly of the antenna masts. Within a few yards of the stile a depression can be seen on the left hand side of the path heading towards Belmont. This marks the route of the collapsed underground tunnel, known as the "New Tunnel" which starts lower down the hill. Just over the wall on the Horwich side – and according to old maps (SD 66356 14536), there used to be an adit or drift entrance to this area of the coal workings but there is very little sign of it today. Near to the site of the adit entrance can be seen many areas of disturbed ground all caused either by surface coal workings or by collapsed workings beneath.

The path along the wall has few surprises except for several spots where rocks appear to be in fairly unnatural formations forming circles.

The above photo on the left is particularly interesting. The original surface of the ground one to two thousand years ago would have been several feet lower than it is today, before the build up of the peat. In those days, these rocks would have been on the lying on the surface and not sunk as at present. I'm not suggesting ancient stone circles ...... but it's an interesting thought!

Whilst I wander on moorlands where I know people once lived in ancient times, as well as looking for flints, I also keep my eyes open for any signs of prehistoric art. This artwork usually consists of either cups, rings or lines carved or cut in rocks. An example of a typical cup and ring boulder was found on the banks of the Lower

Rivington Reservoir just a few years ago and can be seen today outside the Anderton Hall Conference Centre at Horwich.

After years of searching I have so far found no "art" on Winter Hill - or elsewhere in the area! However on the Horwich side of the Dean Ditch wall, I did spot a stone which I thought just "may" have once contained "cups" although with the extreme weathering the rocks have to contend with in this environment, it is doubtful whether any "art" whatsoever would not have been weathered away millennia ago.

Back to the top!

From the TV mast, major footpaths branch in all directions. There are clear paths to Rivington Pike, Noon Hill, Two Lads, Coal Pit Lane and Scout Road to name the main ones. The Scout Road path has already been described and it links into the paths and artefacts described in the Whimberry Hill article. The path to Rivington Pike starts near the cattle grid by the TV mast on the road to Montcliffe and the signposted track to Coal Pit Lane is on the opposite side of the road. You can't miss the Coal Pit track nowadays because of the "paved" footpath for the first few hundred yards of its length

The photo on the left shows a "cup & ring" stone found on the banks of the Rivington Reservoir. It can be seen outside Anderton Hall Conference Centre at Horwich.

Rivington Terraced Gardens.

A guide to their history, vegetation and wildlife.

This article is an amended version of a publication of this name produced by the North West region of the British Trust for Conservation Volunteers in the 1970's. The contents have been amended slightly to protect the exact locations of some of the rarer plant species mentioned. My thanks to BTCV (NW) for allowing this information to be reprinted.

Introduction.

Rivington Terraced Gardens stand out on the hillside below Rivington Pike as an arm of fairly dense woodland, in contrast to the surrounding moorland. A tall tower, "the Dovecote" marks the northern boundary of the gardens which consist of 45 acres of mixed (deciduous and coniferous) woodland. Below the gardens lie Lever Park, north west of which is Rivington Village.

The Historical Development of the gardens.

The area covered by the gardens was was deciduous forest until the early 16th century when it was felled. With grazing and regular burning of the vegetation it became rough grazing moorland, with only a few trees left in the Lower Gardens below what is now Roynton Lane. It remained so until 1900 when William Hesketh Lever bought the site, having enquired whether Liverpool Corporation, who owned the reservoirs in the valley below, were interested and found they were not. Lever was born in Bolton and became wealthy through manufacturing soap from vegetable oil and formed the Unilever Company at Port Sunlight in Cheshire. Landscape design and architecture were among his main interests.

The first building to be erected on the site of the gardens was **"Roynton Cottage"** in 1901. The cottage (or **"Bungalow"** as it is often called) faced west and was built of pine timber and glass. It was designed by Johnathon Simpson, a local architect.

He also designed three lodges to accompany the bungalow between 1901 and 1902 in similar "Victorian Bungalow" style but with thatched roofs. The outline foundations of **South** and **Belmont Lodges** can still be seen. **Bolton Lodge** is the site of the new toilet block. Roynton Lane which passes north through the middle of the gardens was also built at this time.

The original wooden Roynton Cottage circa 1908

In 1905 Lever commissioned **T H Mawson**, a well known landscape architect and former horticulturist, to design the gardens. Thus in the following year the two lawns were laid out – a square one adjacent to the bungalow and an elongated serpentine shaped lawn (the **Great Lawn**) below this. Two garden houses were built overlooking the latter. These can still be seen and are similar in style to the other three garden houses built later. All have unusual circular pillars built of small stones, mullioned windows, and a "terrace" on top with a facade of large stone cross pieces. (Some of the mullions and cross pieces are now missing however.

A **Roman style footbridge** was designed by Lever himself and its large central arch supported six smaller arches can be seen spanning Roynton Lane today.

In 1910 the **"Dovecote"**, probably the most prominent feature of the gardens, was designed by **Robert Atkinson**, together with the adjoining terraces. It consists of 4 rooms, accessible by a spiral stairway. The high-pitched roof, curving outwards from its base is an unusual feature of the tower. It was restored in 1976 according to the original design at the NW Water Authority's expense. Adjacent to the Dovecote (also used as a lookout tower) is a wall with arched windows in. Some of these have large stone slabs against them with holes that are semi-circular in shape. These enabled the doves or pigeons to fly in and out of the shed which originally occupied the site between the wall and the road.

Also in 1910 the **Gatehouse**, which spanned Roynton Lane with a hexagonal building at each end was built. It was demolished in the 50's but the two circular stone gateposts and foundations can still be seen. In 1913 Roynton Cottage was burnt down by Suffragettes to demonstate against "use of capital". It was timed to coincide with a visit by George V and Queen Mary. It was replaced the following year by a more "fire proof" house of local stone (millstone grit) and

glass. Although only a one-story building, the **New Bungalow** was ornate particularly inside – on the dining room ceiling for instance was painted the position of the constellations on October the 23rd 1851, the day Lever was born. The First World War delayed part of the proposed building – an elaborate circular ballroom was not completed until 1920. The garden house in the north west of the gardens was also built at about this time.

In 1919 the gardens were opened to the public for the first time. Work on the gardens was begun again in the 1920's following its delay by the first world war. Many paths were laid out with irregular crazy paving, and flightsof stone steps and archways constructed. The **Japanese Gardens** with a waterfall, large lagoon, garden ornaments and shelters, built to resemble Japanese tea houses, were completed. Also at this time the **Italian Gardens** were created.. A series of waterfalls and ponds were formed by diverting a small stream, and four inter-connecting caves were made partly by excavation and partly by construction. Rock ledges and steep pathways were made adjacent to the stream and two footbridges also crossed it. As in other parts of the gardens use was made of the horizontally-layered local rock.

In 1925 **Lord Leverhulme**, as he had then become, (having attached his wifes name to his own) died. The large death duties that his son, Vicount Leverhulme, subsequently had to pay, forced him to sell the various properties and to sack the 50 landscape gardeners hired from London and 50 local workmen that worked in the gardens. **John Magee**, a local brewery owner, bought the bungalow and grounds but the latter were kept open to the public and the bungalow was opened annually until his death in 1939. Even before Magee's death the gardens became neglected presumable because he could not afford to maintain them, and after his death and with the Second World War the situation became worse.

Leverhulme's footbridge over Roynton Lane
Liverpool Corporation bought the land from the Magee family, the local authorities being unable to afford it, despite Magee's wishes. During the 1939-45 war Rivington Bungalow was acquired by the army and much damage was done – the glass roof of the ballroom was smashed and the floor was ripped up. Vandalism became a problem generally in the Gardens. The cost of repairing and

maintaining the buildings led to Liverpool Corporation's decision to demolish the Bungalow and the three lodges in 1948, after various other uses had been considered (including a hospital) and despite objections from local people. Today a small black and white tiled area can be seen on the Bungalow site but little else remains.

Nearby lie the **Kitchen Gardens**, their dividing walls still fairly high. Greenhouses once occupied the two northernmost walled areas. Further south, the **Potting Shed** can still be seen with the walls virtually intact, although they have long since lost their roofs. Opposite the Kitchen Gardens is the outline of a **Pagoda or Japanese teahouse** can be seen, adjacent to the ruins of a small garage. There was another garage further north which had a dovecote on top. The foundations and large building stones can still be seen here. Inset in the wall adjacent to the path near here are stone built shelters which contained wooden seats. These can be seen in several places in the Gardens next to the paths.

Since the 1970's beneficial changes have taken place in the Gardens, voluntary conservation groups have cleared the once overgrown paths and ponds and restored some of the stonework, so that people can enjoy the Gardens more fully and a variety of plants and animals can co-exist. *(this description does not give full credit to the massive amount of work done by the British Trust for Conservation Volunteers who totally transformed the Gardens from a total overgrown jungle to the beauty we now enjoy today, thanks!)*

Vegetation and Wildlife.

Introduction

Many different species were planted in the Gardens and many of them have survived despite the physical conditions. The soil is acid, the rainfall rather heavy (about 45 inches a year), and as the site is on a steep slope (from 220 to 320 metres above sea level) rather strong winds occur at times. Some species have been lost, through neglect and the rapid spread of some plants, at the expense of others, and theft. However over 150 of plants have been identified in the Gardens at the present time (May 1978).

In a short article such as this, only a brief account of such a variety of species can be given. The location of some of the plants is indicated by numbers in brackets which refer to the map.

Trees.

A large number of different trees can be seen in the gardens – there are about 40 species about which half are conifers , the rest being broadleaved. All the broadleaved ones are deciduous (i.e. lose all their leaves in winter) apart from **Griselinia**. Most of the tree species present are not native to this country. Some, such as the Monkey Puzzle (1), come from as far away as South America. There is a noticeable difference in the trees of the Lower and those of the Upper Gardens. In the latter, there are more exotic species, particularly conifers, as this area was treeless moorland until 1905, the oldest trees being therefore 98 years old *(in 2003)*.

Oak, Birch and Rowan are the most common deciduous **broadleaved trees**. Others are infrequently seen: **Elm** (2), **Willow** (3), **Alder** (4), **Whitebeam** (5), **Ash** and **Wild Cherry** are noticeable near the paths through the gardens. A cultivated variety of Ash, **"Weeping Ash"**, with drooping branches can be seen near the Japanese Lagoon.

Sycamore, introduced into this country in the 17th Century, has spread rapidly in the gardens and in the Lower Gardens particularly, the vast numbers of seedlings it is able to produce can be seen very frequently. Considerable numbers of Sycamores have been felled by Conservation Volunteers to allow other species to grow, especially native deciduous trees such as Oak. These generally have many other plants associated with them , dependent on them for food and shelter.

Beech is a common tree in the gardens, and in addition to the Common Beech there are two other varieties: **Copper Beech** with its dark purple leaves and **Cut-Leaf Beech** (7).

Exotic Cherry trees are also fairly common in the kitchen garden area. They have smooth shiny reddish bark and produce prolific blossom in summer.

Other introduced broadleaved trees present but rare in the gardens are,: **Lime, Horse Chestnut, Norway Maple, Laburnum** (a poinenous tree with long tassels of yellow flowers), and the **False Acacia or Locust Tree** (8). The latter is an unusual tree with rough channelled bark and paired spines on the twigs, pinnate leaves resembling Ash, and white flowers drooping like Laburnum. There are only two of these trees in the gardens.

Griselinia Littoralis (9) is another unusual and interesting tree found only in one place in the gardens. It comes from New Zealand and has evergreen untoothed leaves, bright and shiny above but dull below.

Conifers.

These are identifiable by their narrow, needle-like leaves and the fact that they bear cones. **Larch** is the only deciduous conifer and occurs in considerable numbers in the gardens (10).

Several species of **Pines** (Pinus spp.) are present, the most common ones (all of which have needles in pairs) are:- **Scots Pine** (with blue-green needles about 1.5 inches long), is very common particularly in the Lower Gardens. **Corsican Pine** has needles about 4 inches long; there are some large specimens by the south west garden house. **Mountain Pine** (pinus mungo) is a small bushy pine with many bright green needles grouped in whorls on the branches (unlike other pines), the bare twig can be seen between the whorls. This pine occurs in large numbers near the seven arch bridge.

Another group of conifers are the **Spruces** which have very sharply pointed, short stiff needles growing singly on small woody pegs which are left when the needles fall, thus the twigs are very rough when touched. **Sitka Spruce** is the most common, the underside of its needles are blue-grey. There are only three or four **Blue Spruce** trees (12) but they are easily noticeable as their needles are blue-grey all over, and they point in all directions from the twigs.

Silver Firs (Abies spp.) are quite common in the gardens – their needles are set in two distinct layers, the lower ones being horizontal so that the foliage looks flattened. The needles grow singly (unlike the paired needles of the pines) and leave a flat round scar when removed unlike the Spruces. The bark is dark and not channelled, but has small resin bubbles on it. Three very tall Silver Firs can be seen by the SW summerhouse (13).

Cedars (14) have needles set in tufts or dense bunches like larches but they are of different lengths and remain over winter. Also their cones may be 8 cms long whereas those of larch are only 2 or 3 cms long. Only three ceder trees have been found in the gardens but all are adjacent to paths.

There are several **Cypress** (Chamaecyparis) trees in the gardens, their flattened spreading foliage of tiny leaves which overlap the stem, make them unlike any of the conifers mentioned above.

Another conifer which has overlapping small leaves but which does not have flattened spreading branches is **Cryptomeria japonica** (15) of which there is only one tree in the gardens.

Yew is the only native conifer besides Scots Pine present in the gardens, here it grows as a small bushy tree particularly between the kitchen gardens and the Japanese Lagoon. The leaves are soft to touch and often yellowish-green.

Shrubs.

Introduction.
Mawson planted thousands of **Rhododendrons** and many other shrubs including **Gaultheria, Kalmias, Vaccineums, Hollies, Berberis** and many others. Some of these species originally planted are no longer present, having been lost through theft and neglect with some shrubs such as **Rhododendron, Gaultheria** and **Pernettya** spreading rapidly at the expense of other species. However 29 different shrub plants are to be found in the gardens today, nearly all of them introduced species, some of them fairly rare. Many of the shrubs planted appear to have been chosen because of their hardiness and tolerance of, or even preference for, an acid soil, e.g. many members of the **Ericaceae (Heather)** family and Rhododendron. The latter, together with Gaultheria and Pernettya, are the most common shrubs in the gardens, having spread rapidly by means of underground suckers. A number of varieties of Rhododendron are present, all characterised by untoothed leathery leaves and trumpet shaped flowers of various colours. Some of them have unusually small leaves (only 0.75 inches wide and 2 inches long but the most common is **Rhododendron ponticum** with large tough dark green leaves. The **deciduous Azeleas** occur in several places in the gardens.

Pernettya mucronata, aptly called **"Prickly Heath"** is a shrub growing up to about 2 foot high with small toothed leaves alternately arranged on its red stem. Introduced from the extreme south of South USA, it is evergreen (like Gaultheria) and bears red berries.

Oleria hastii (16) is an unusual shrub from New Zealand and is found adjacent to the summerhouses in the Upper Gardens. It has curiously stringy bark and untoothed evergreenleaves which are felty and buff coloured underneath. In July/August it bears daisy like flowers – thus it is included in the group of shrubs called the "Daisy Bushes".

Bamboo (17), a plant found naturally in S E Asia is a plant one would not expect to find growing here but there are several plants in the Italian Gardens.

Above the swimming pool are two small **Quince** (18) bushes and adjacent to the square lawn by the bungalow site you can see the only site where **Dogwood Cornel** grows in the Gardens (19). It is a deciduous shrub easily recognised by its bright red stems and shoots.

At least two species of **Laurel** occur in the Gardens:- "Spotted Laurel" with yellow spots on its leaves, and the "Common" or "Cherry Laurel" with its large glossy evergreen leaves with prominent veins.

Holly is a fairly common shrub or small tree in the gardens and species present are: Broad Leaved Holly (whose leaves are up to 2 inches across) and the **Common Holly** of which there is also a variegated (yellow-margined) variety occurring here.

Two species of **Barberry (Berberis spp.)**, a very spiny shrub up to three feet high, can be found in the gardens. **"Rosemary Barberry" (Berberis stenophylla)** with small inrolled untoothed leaves, grows well in places, particularly near the Great Lawn. The other has small holly-like leaves and grows in only a few places. **Pieris taiwanensis** (20) grows abundantly above the Japanese Lagoon and is one of the first shrubs to flower in the gardens. It produces abundant white, lily-of-the-valley type flowers in early April, and has alternately arranged leaves, distinguished from small rhododerons by their finely toothed edges, pale green colour and narrowly lanceclata (spear-like) shape.

Also in the early spring **Flowering Current** bushes are noticeable with their drooping red flowers unlike the **Red Current** (found in the Kitchen Gardens) which has insignificant greenish-yellow flowers. Other typical vegetable garden plants growing here include **Gooseberry**.

The other shrubs likely to be seen are native to the area, although some of them may have been planted: **Elder, Hawthorne, Hazel and Gorse.**

Ground Flora. (Flowers, grasses, rushes, ferns, mosses etc)

Although there are large areas of the gardens where there is little ground vegetation, particularly where not much light penetrates the tree and shrub leaf-canopy, a large variety of plants (over 70 species) are present. Although Mawson originally planted introduced species such as Alpine varieties, most of the ground vegetation now consists of native species that one would expect to find growing naturally in this area.

Some of these are typically English woodland plants e.g. **Bluebell** and various grasses, particularly the soft hairy **Holcus species** which are very common in the gardens; and **Wood Sage** and **Wood Sorrel** which are relatively rare. Others typically colonise bare ground; **Sheeps Sorrel, Chickweeds,** the small **Annual Meadow Grass** with its bright green leaves with keeled tips, and **Foxglove** all grow well on waste ground, on the edges of the paths and on slopes of otherwise bare soil (Particularly following Rhododendron clearance).

Other plants are characteristic moorland species; **Heather, Bilberry, Heath Bedstraw, Mat Grass, Flying Bent Grass and rushes**. In some places, such as the Great Lawn, they have re-colonised the area again. Of the **Rushes (Juncus spp.), Soft Rush** is the most common, forming large tufts about a foot high, and the smaller **Heath Rush** is common on the lawns. It is generally less than 9 inches high, does not form tufts and has small narrow leaves at its base. All the plants are abundant on the moorland surrounding the gardens.

Other plants are typically found in wet places – in or by the streams, ponds and boggy areas in the gardens: **Water Forget-me-Not, Marsh Thistle, Bittercress, Iris and Reed Sweet Grass (Glyceria maxima).** The latter has bluntly pointed folded leaves that may be 1 inch wide and grows up to several feet. It is found in "Neptunes

Pool" (21). The flat basal rosettes of leaves of **Hairy Bittercress** are common especially near the stream in the Italian Garden.

Japanese Knotweed (Reynoutria japonica) is a Japanese species planted in the gardens and has spread rapidly by means of underground suckers. It is a tall, stout cane-like plant growing up to 6 feet high with large oval leaves and tassels of white flowers in summer.

Of particular interest are plants confined to the stone walls of the terraces and summerhouses in the gardens such as **Ivy and Berrillio Sandwort,** a tiny plant which produces relatively large white flowers in April. **Ivy-leaved Toadflax** which has purple flowers , can be seen growing on the seven arched bridge. **Epilobium nerteriodes** is a small creeping willow herb with round leaves introduced from New Zealand but which now grows wld in the UK. The plant grows well on the rock faces by the interconnecting caves in the Italian Gardens. Here also the moist shady conditions provide an ideal habitat for **mosses, the flat green liverworts,** and some Ferns, particularly **Lady Fern**. The ferns most frequently seen in the gardens are **Bracken, Broad Buckler Fern and Lady Fern**, which are common particularly in the Lower Gardens. **Hard Fern** with its lobed fronds only a few inches long, occurs in several places.

Animals.

The variety of plants and presence and shrubs offer food and shelter for many animals that otherwise would not be found here.

Birds.
Thirty species of birds have been identified. They include birds of prey such as the Owl and Kestrel; typical woodland birds like the Great Spotted Woodpecker and Wood Pigeon. Some birds such as the Goldcrest (a very small bird with a golden-yellow stripe on top of its head) have benefited from the planting of conifers in the gardens, preferring to nest in them rather than in deciduous trees.

The birds most likely to be seen apart from the above species are: Robin, Blackbird, Blue-, Great-, and Coal Tits, Magpie, and Chaffinch, Wren and Tree Creeper. The latter is noted for its habit of creeping up tree trunks looking for insects and its prominent white front in contrast to its mottled brown back. Other species present include Bullfinch, Redstart, Redpoll, Jay, Starling, Hedge Sparrow, Chiff-chaff, Carrion Crow, Cuckoo, Linnet, Fieldfare, Nuthatch, Long Tailed Tit, Willow Warbler and Redwing.

Mammals & Amphibians.

Rabbits, Hedgehog, Wood Mice, Fox, Weasel and Stoat have been seen and recorded in the gardens but only the rabbit is a common sight. Frogs and Smooth Newts are the only amphibians to have been seen in the gardens.

Please Remember:-

A lot of time, energy and money has been spent (and will continue to be spent) trying to conserve the variety of features in the gardens which make them interesting for the large numbers of people that visit them now and in the future. In some cases damage and erosion has occurred, therefore for everyone's benefit PLEASE:
- be careful not to start a fire
- don't drop litter
- keep to the paths so plants are not damaged and wildlife is not disturbed
- don't damage walls and buildings
- keep to approved vehicle/bike routs and car parks.

BTCV (North West Region), Oakham Court, Averham Lane, Preston, PR1 3XP, Lancashire. Telephone: 01772 204647 Fax: 01772 257106

++

Bolton Mountain Rescue Team.

A bit about what we do and where we operate

Primarily, we exist to provide a voluntary search and rescue service for the West Pennine Moors, but besides searching for missing or injured hill walkers and people involved in mountain biking and climbing accidents, (which is usually the first thing pictured when the phrase "mountain rescue" is mentioned) we are also heavily involved in other happenings.

Our past callouts have involved crashed aircraft, hang gliders and parapenters. Generally, however, where there is a problem locating victims, or the terrain surrounding a casualty is difficult to access, it is likely that your mountain rescue team is involved.

Several times a year we also provide standby rescue cover for events held within our area. We can often be spotted at orienteering events, fell races, sponsored walks, and mountain bike races.

We are a key resource to the emergency services, our specialist skills being recognised and respected by Greater Manchester, Lancashire and Cheshire police who utilise us (along with other teams) to help in search and rescue operations, alongside use by the Ambulance services. The team also works with Greater Manchester Fire Service.

Besides our upland moorland area, we also operate throughout the lowland areas of Bolton, Salford, Wigan, Trafford, Manchester South, and the western half of Bury. We are also called upon to assist other teams in North Manchester, the eastern half of Bury, Tameside, Rochdale, Oldham, North Cheshire and South Lancashire.

Image property of Bolton Mountain Rescue Team.

A little bit of history

Founded in 1968 by 3 Rossendale Fell Rescue Team members, who lived in the Bolton area, the Team has grown from its small beginnings to be one of the busiest and best equipped teams in the country.

The early years, as with many foundling organisations, was one of sheer hard work to raise minimal amounts of money for essential equipment which was initially transported both for exercise and incidents in privately owned vehicles.

The first vehicles owned by the Team were all old "second-hand" ones past their best before date, they were cherished and nursed by the dedicated membership. Much is owed to these early pioneers, most of whom have long left but two remain in the team - Alan "General" James, one of the original founder members, now a life Vice President, only stopped active service in early 1999 due to a job move to the London area. Geoffrey H. Seddon, currently Deputy Team Leader, joined within a few months of the Team's inauguration and has served as Team Leader (7 years) and Chairman.

The 1980's saw consolidation of the Team with a gradual improvement in the quality and quantity of equipment and vehicles. During this decade we saw the implementation of structured training and the MRC casualty care course and certificate. By the late 80's and early 90's, training was based on a professional and formalised activity.

As a "fringe" Mountain Rescue Team based in an rural/urban area, the local moorlands generated few incidents. Even up until the early 90's fewer than 10 incidents per year were the norm. In the 70's and 80's 2 or 3 call outs per year were common.

The combination of a large urban catchment area for membership and low incident rate meant a very high level of training was able to be undertaken. Morale was maintained by training weekends in the Lakes or North Wales with the added bonus of possible calls to assist local teams. Langdale Ambleside MRT (Stewart Hulse MBE, Team Leader) and Ogwen Valley MRT (Tony Jones, Team Leader) were especially supportive and encouraging.

The advent of the West Pennine Moors Recreation Area, coupled with years of liaison meetings with the Lancashire and Greater

Manchester Police Forces and the Lancashire and Greater Manchester Ambulance Services saw a dramatic rise in call out activity from 1994 onwards as the professional expertise and resources of the team were recognised on a wider basis. We can now expect upwards of 100 incidents attended by the team per year.

1999 also saw the team with its very first new vehicles - 2 Landrover 110" County Station Wagons and a Landrover 110" hardtop. The first two being first response vehicles and the hardtop van an Incident Support Unit. The team also utilises an ex-Ambulance as a Personnel Carrier.

++

Geological Walk. The River Douglas North of Horwich.
By Rodney J Ireland.

(This was, I believe just one of a number of walks around the area contained in a booklet published by the Wigan Geological Society - which seems to no longer exist.. I have been unable to obtain a full copy of this booklet, merely a photocopy of this article)

Introduction.

The excursion, which follows the course of the RiverDouglas, commences at Rivington School, Lever Park Avenue, Horwich and terminates on Rivington Pike. Most of the journey is made along the river bed itself in order to see the best exposures. It is therefore recommended that, if possible, wellington boots are worn. Although the walking distance between the school and the Pike is only 1.5 miles (3 kilometres) the valley is steep and travelling over much rough ground. Accordingly, it is recommended that the better part of the day is set aside for the excursion. It is also recommended that the excursion should not be attempted immediately following heavy rainfall since high flows in the river can result in the route being dangerous and, furthermore, renders several exposures inaccessible.

Despite the above cautionary notes, the excursion is both worthwhile and interesting. The valley affords numerous excellent exposures of the Lower Coal Measures (Westphalian) and Millstone Grit Series (Namurian). The geomorphology and faulting is also noteworthy and, in clear weather, a final reward is provided by the panoramic views from the Pike.

Itinerary.

Rivington School (SD 638127), may be reached by following Lever Park Avenue out of Horwich for a distance of about 1 km. There is ample parking space alongside the Avenue in the vicinity of the school. Take the footpath leading east from the south side of the large Sports Hall alongside the road. The footpath leads to Old Lords Farm Footbridge (639126). Hereabouts, upstream from the bridge, leave the footpath, climb through one of the gaps in the old iron fence, descend to the river bed and proceed upstream.

In the river banks and on the bed, exposures of shales, mudstones and siltstones with occasional thin sandstones (less than 0.2 metre) can be seen. These rocks form part of the strata between the Crutchman Sandstone and the Old Lawrence Rock (sandstone) within the Lower Coal Measures. Carefully note the stratal dips. Initially the beds are horizontal but some 200 metres upstream the same beds can be seen dipping at 20 degrees. Careful examination of the siltstone/mudstone sequences hereabouts reveals the presence of fossil plant debris. Another 10 metres upstream the siltstones, dipping even more steeply, are abruptly truncated by a fault. This can be clearly seen on the south side of the river and trends in a north-westerly direction. The fault surface contains a fault breccia consisting of angular pieces of sanstone and siltstone occurring within a matrix of sand and mud. The hade, or slope of the fault surface, indicates a south-westerly downthrow. Upstream the Ousel Nest Grit (or Horwich Grit) and its underlying shales and occasional flagstones are exposed. The stratal juxtaposition indicates a vertical displacement on the fault of about 250 metres. The increasing dips observed downstream are features common to many such displacements.

Continue upstream from the fault. Siltstones and occasional flaggy sandstones, both both much disturbed by the fault, can be seen. There, considerable variation in stratal dip and some folding also occurs. Above a small waterfall, the beds become horizontal again. Black and purple shales and siltstones crop out on the left bank of the river and become overturned at the waterfall. Such overturning is probably the result of "soil creep". Some 15 to 20 metres upstream from the waterfall a coarse-grained yellow sandstone (Ousel Nest Grit) can be seen. Many small faults with slickensides (the polished fault surface exhibiting striations which indicate the last direction of movement) are present. One fault, exposed on the right bank, throws shales against sandstones. For approximately the next 40 metres, the river is in a very narrow, steep sided and picturesque ravine containing a series of cascades and waterfalls. It is possible to traverse the ravine and observe the Ousel Nest Grit which is subject to much small faulting with associated well developed slickensides. However if you are not wearing wellingtons be prepared to get your feet wet!. Alternatively a detour around the ravine may be made, leaving the river bed and rejoining the river upstream. A small quarry on the right bank above the ravine displays a particularly well-exposed fault surface exhibiting white slickensides. Further upstream observe the feature created by the Ousel Nest Grit on the left bank. Here the sandstone is well-jointed and cross-stratification can be demonstrated. As the footbridge is approached note the sandstone is terminated against shales. Here again, faulting can be demonstrated.

Immediately upstream from here a careful examination of the 1 metre of mudstone and shale, overlying the compact, dark, flaggy sandstone in the river bed, reveals the presence of a Marine Band. This is best exposed on the right bank below the roots of a large tree. Goniatites (*Gastrioceras*), bivalves (*Dunbarella*) and brachiopods (*Lingula*) can be readily found. Most of the goniatites are flattened by the compactation of the sediments. However, detailed inspection shows them to be *Gastriocerous subcrenatum*. Some excavation below the Marine Band shows the presence of a thin inferior coal (0.015 metre), and immediately above this the non-marine bivalve *Anthraconaia bellula* has been found. The fossils prove the coal to be the Six Inch Mine at the base of the Lower Coal Measures. The former is separated by some 60 metres of stata from the overlying Ousel Nest Grit. Since the two horizons are faulted into juxtaposition immediately downstream of the footbridge, the throw of the fault must therefore be approximately 60 metres.

Continuing upstream, a high wall, the remains of an old dam, is passed on the left bank. A series of "terraced" sandy gravels clearly represents the partial infill of a former mill "lodge" impounded by the dam.

Upstream the valley bifurcates. Both tributaries enter over waterfalls caused by a north-westerly trending fault throwing the shales and mudstones, above the Six Inch Mine, against the Upper Haslingden Flags. The hard flagstones are resistant to erosion and hence form the lip of the waterfall. The shales and the mudstones on the downthrown side of the fault are soft and have been eroded to form "plunge pools" at the base of the falls. Take the left hand tributary, ascend around the waterfall and return to the stream bed. Here the river gradient coincides with the dip of the bedding surfaces in the Upper Haslingden Flags. Accordingly, one walks on a single bedding surface for some considerable distance. Sedimentary structures, including ripple marks, may be seen on the bedding surfaces. Joint frequency and direction may also be examined. (Great care is required as hereabouts much of the river bed is **very slippery**). Near the top of the gorge the overlying shales crop out and rest on the top of the flagstones. Above here, the base of the Rough Rock, a feldspathic sandstone, and the highest member of the Millstone Grit Series can be examined.

At the top of the gorge it is necessary to again climb through the old boundary fence. Upstream the stream bed is incised in the Rough Rock which, between the fence and Belmont Road, exhibits several well-developed pot holes. Above and left of the stream two slope changes can be seen on the hillside. These represent the outcrops of the Upper and Lower leaves of the Sand Rock Mine. Both coal seams occur within the Rough Rock. However, only the upper seam was of workable thickness. Spoil heaps can be seen beneath Brown Hill where a drift mine formerly worked the coal. Crossing Belmont Road and continuing upstream, well developed cross-stratification occurs in the Rough Rock.

From here traverse due West towards Brown Hill. Immediately east of the hill a northerly trending fault is visible in the small stream. The fault truncates the Rough Rock and throws down the overlying shales. From the steam climb up the side of Brown Hill where the shales pass upwards into the Margery Flags. These form the capping of the hill and dip at 8 degrees to the south. Descend Brown Hill on the north-west side towards Rivington Pike. In the saddle between the two hills, and to the right of the track, a circular depression with a surrounding raised lip can be seen. This probably represents an old bell pit which worked the Sand Rock Mine. From here it is well worth completing the excursion by walking to the top of Rivington Pike. There are several limited exposures of the Marjory Flags en route.

From the Pike one can return to the School by descending through the plantations and the terraced gardens to Rivington Barn. Alternatively a more direct route may be followed by descending across the fields to Roynton Lane and thence to the rear of the school.

References.
JONES R C B et al (1938) Wigan District   Mem. Geol> Surv

Maps
Geological (IGS)
1:63,360 (1 in to 1 ml) Sheet No 84 – Wigan (solid)
1:10,560 (6 in to 1 ml) Lancs. Sheet No 86 NW
Ordnance Survey
1:50,000 Series, Sheet 109
1:10,560 Series, Sheet SD 61 SW

Good Friday. The Pike Fair.

Good Friday at Rivington Pike is either a nightmare or a pleasurable annual event, dependent on how you see things. For me, it's a nightmare yet I still keep going back every Good Friday … and now I even go with my grandchildren!

Good Friday is the day of the "Pike Fair". On that day each year, the "fair" arrives at the Pike along with hot dog vans, children's entertainment's complete with bouncy castles and tacky stalls selling all sorts of things that we don't really want. At the end of the day when all the traders have gone, the Pike area looks something like a giant rubbish dump. It must be the only "fair" in the country to be held near the top of a fairly inhospitable hill whatever the weather!

Nobody really seems to know when the Pike Fair originated, but it is undoubtedly of fairly ancient origin, possibly dating from the Middle Ages. It used to be held at the Whitsuntide weekend and in the early 1800's the fair seems to have been a rather rowdy event and - according to a local newspaper – the road round the Pike was filled with "nut stalls and drinking booths". Add to this, the proximity of the public house, the Sportsman's Arms, just a few hundred yards from the Pike and it must have been quite a lively spot especially as the festivities lasted from the Saturday morning, through the night, through the Sunday finally closing on the Monday! Sunday was the day when people from all around always walked to the peak of Rivington Pike – and still do.

After The Sportsman's Arms lost its licence (I don't know the exact date or the reason but I believe it occurred around 1880), the fair seemed to calm down and local interest in it began to wane. An article in the Bolton Chronicle of 1884 commented that "Pike Fair has lost much of its rowdyism since the removal of the public house licence"

The fair was moved to Good Friday in 1900 and since that time the numbers of stalls and visitors have fluctuated wildly decade by decade. According to one article I have read, it would seem that things were fairly quiet in the 1930's and 40's but by the 1960's, crowds of over 50,000 were reported (along with increasing crowd and litter problems). Nowadays, the fair seems much quieter than I remember it 20 years ago and the number of stalls is well down in numbers.

So why do I keep going to the fair if it that's awful? Pure habit and I love things that are a bit out of the ordinary – especially when it's a tradition.

Aerial view of the Pike, taken prior to the building of the southern "staircase". The photo is taken from my microlight flying about 800 feet above the Pike

Rivington Pike and the Tower.

When driving along the motorway past Horwich, two things immediately catch the eye, the Reebok Stadium and the Tower on Rivington Pike. I wonder how many thousands of people have driven past and wondered what the Tower is? Many local history books tell you all you could ever want to know about the Tower but any book about Winter Hill would be incomplete without a few words about the Pike and its Tower so I'll try to give a potted version of what you'll find in the other books.

Rivington Pike is the last high point at the south western edge of Winter Hill and is 1,198 ft or 365 metres high. A surveyors bench mark can be seen carved onto one of the large boulders halfway up the Pike on the main footpath leading from the Brown Hill area. Geologically the Pike is composed of gritstones, shales and several layers of the Margery Flags. The Pike is circled by two coal outcrops – but they are fairly speculative on the eastern side, although coal has been extracted there in days gone by.

There are three major routes up the Pike, the Brown Hill footpath, the paths from Winter Hill and that from the Terraced Gardens. There is a road going round the hill. Due to the erosion occurring on the Terraced Gardens Path (which was getting quite severe with the footpath forming an ever-deepening gully) a staircase was built up the Pike in latter years.

The summit of the Pike was once the site of a beacon. The first recorded use of it was in the 12th century when those awful Scottish people invaded our part of the UK. At that time, the whole country was linked with a chain of fire beacons to alert the population in times of crisis. Apart from this occurrence, there seems to be only one other record of the beacon chain being lit in anger, this being on the 19th July 1588 when the Spanish Armada threatened our shores. The beacon was held in readiness for lighting at a time in the early 1800's when a French invasion was threatened, but the beacon was never lit. The beacon site has only been used since that time on the odd occasion to celebrate war victories or royal occasions.

The Tower.

The builder of the tower on Winter Hill was John Andrews in 1733 and it is reputed that he built it as a sign of his authority and ownership following an earlier land dispute with another landowner. The tower was built to function as a shooting hut and initially consisted of one square room with a cellar underneath. One source says that the room was oak panelled and there was definitely a fireplace within the walls as early photos clearly show a chimney on the roof. There was one door into the tower with windows in the other three sides. The roof was below the level of the walls and could not be seen from the outside. The stones for building the tower were obtained locally and those from the original beacon were utilised in the structure.

The Pike as it used to be (photo taken in 1979) before the building of the "grand staircase". The erosion was a great deal worse than this by the time the new steps were built.

Photo of the tower taken in the 1880's. Note the chimney!

In the 1890's, Rivington Hall and the surrounding lands were bought for £60,000 by William Lever - Vicount Leverhulme - who was a Boltonian who had made his fortune in soap manufacturing starting the company that was to end up as Unilever. After Levers death he bequeathed his lands to the "people of Bolton" on condition that it was preserved as a park with total public access. Liverpool Corporation objected to parts of this bequest as portions of the land lay within the Liverpool Waterworks water catchment area. As a result of various court cases, Parliament decreed that although the park remained as a gift to the people of Bolton, the property would be managed by Liverpool Corporation. As a result of this arrangement the tower started to fall into a state of disrepair.

Although Liverpool made general repairs to the structure from time to time, no real attempt seems to have been made to make it really presentable and in 1967 they announced that they intended to demolish the tower. Following massive local objections to this course of action which lasted for some years the ownership of the land was sold to Chorley UDC and the tower was finally repaired in 1973.

RIVINGTON PIKE AND TOWER. GOOD FRIDAY APRIL 13th 1979.

A few lesser known facts about Rivington Pike!

Vegetation.

The vegetation composition of the Pike is what is known as a "semi-natural upland acidic grassland environment" and is said to be "anthropogenic" i.e man modified. Without mans interference (and sheep!) heather, bracken and scrubby plants would soon colonise the land and trees would start to regenerate naturally.

So what types of plants are actually growing on and around the Pike? By far the most dominant grass is Nardus Stricta (Mat Grass), but Molinia Caerulea (Purple Moor Grass/Flying Bent) becomes especially abundant in the southern half of the site, especially in the wetter south-western corner. Other plant species noticeably present are:

Festus ovina (Sheeps Fescue)
Deschampsia flexuosa (Wavy Hair Grass)
Agrostis canina montana (Brown Bent)
Poa annua (Annual Meadow Grass)
Agrostis tenuis (Common Bent/Brown Top)
Cynosurus cristatus (Crested Dog's Tail)
Juncus squarrosus (Heath/Moor Rush)
Juncus conglomeratus (Common Rush)
Vaccinium myrtillus (Bilberry)
Empetrum nigrum (Crowberry)
Callauna vulgaris (Heather)
Epiophorum vaginatum (Hare's Tail Cotton Grass).

The weather.

Due to its exposed and high elevation, the Pike does experience severe weather conditions with the prevailing strong winds coming from the west. Rainfall is heavy and frequent. Measurements were taken in 1977 and during that year a total rainfall of 1169 mm (approx. 46 inches was recorded. No month by month rainfall figures have been recorded for the Pike but they are available for Brown

Hill, a few hundred yards to the south east. These show that the monthly rainfall throughout 1977 was:

January	79.2mm
February	157.0
March	70.0
April	79.2mm
May	46.5
June	161.5
July	38.5
August	73.2
September	89.0
October	124.3
November	151.8
December	98.9

(source NWWA)

The Pike Geology.

"The underlying solid geology of the Pike is Carboniferous in age. Beds of the Millstone Grit Series are overlain by "marine bands" and Margery Flags. The latter here represents the base of the sandstones and grits of the Lower Coal Measures. The Carboniferous rocks are strongly bedded and generally sandstone and shales alternate. The rocks dip only very slightly to the south-east"

"The sudden rise of the land to form the oval shaped ridge on which the Tower stands can be partly explained by the Lower Coal Measures present which are also oval in shape, and the base coincides approximately with the 351 metre contour. At the summit of the Pike, some of the bedrock has been exposed and strongly bedded, fine grained, vertically jointed sandstone can be seen to be underlain by very easily disturbed thin shale bands which are readily fragmented."

The Soil.

"The soil profile generally consists of, in decending order: a thin layer of humus; a layer of peat which varies in thickness; a bleached, greyed, browny, clayey, very acidic alluvial horizon containing small fragments of sandstone and shale; a thin iron pan; a relatively thick, partly iron stained, darker brown, less clayey, more sandy alluvial horizon within which are larger fragments of sandstone and shale; the parent rock.

Extracts taken from "Rivington Pike. Erosion and Management Plan" by Christine Tudor for BTCV and NWWA . June 1978.

++

The Hole Bottom Area of Winter Hill.

"Hole Bottom". What a name! Don't expect me to explain why the place has this name because I haven't a clue! If anyone has any explanation then please get in touch then we can all share this invaluable and fascinating information!

90% of people reading this are going to ask where Hole Bottom is! It's no wonder you don't know where it is, for today it's one of the most insignificant spots on Winter Hill and is totally ignored by most walkers and drivers unless you happen to be a "local". To find the place, go up the road leading to the TV mast from Montcliffe, go over the cattle grid and eventually you'll reach a left bend in the road with a metal crash barrier on the right side of the road. This is Hole Bottom! Welcome to one of the most fascinating spots on the hill!

If you stand at Hole Bottom and look around, what do you see? Not much ………… for little now remains of what was once here. This was once a thriving, working small community with a brick & tile works, coal mines, houses (including an ale house – wish it were still there) and was on a major route from one part of the county to another. If you look carefully at the photo below, there are clues to the past history. Look uphill towards the mast. Over a century ago you would have seen a number of pit heads all the way up to the present TV mast. There is a clear track leading up the hill that was once a tramway. Also on the hillside looking uphill there are a large number of blocked remains of adit entrances and a number of "collapsed" areas where the underground coal and clay workings have fallen in.

In the small "valley" to the right of the photo, there used to be three major adits leading from the valley into the Mountain Mine coal workings. Two of these adits are now completely filled in and sealed, and the third one seems to have been commandeered by the water department as the entrance is covered by a modern brick built structure (which is just about visible from the road as it's surrounded by a fence).

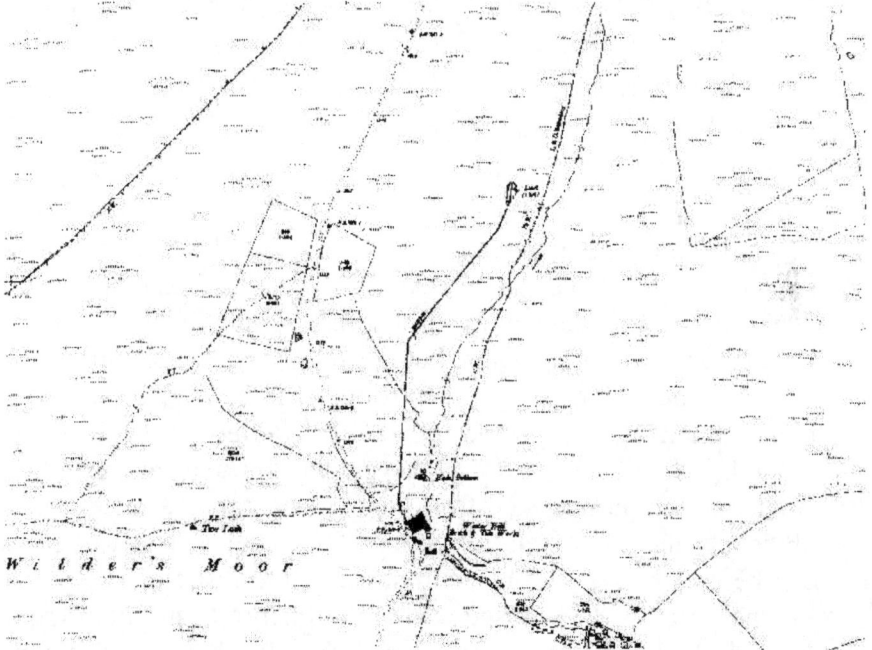

To the right of the photo and directly behind the crash barrier is the site of the old Winter Hill Brick & Tile works, now demolished. Less than 100 yards higher up the road on the left hand side there used to be a row of houses called "Five Houses". The Five Houses appear on many old maps of the area but are not shown on the 1894 First Edition maps.

The brick works were probably once known as "Five Houses Fire Brick and Tile works" as can be seen from an advert in the Bolton Chronicle on the 19th February 1849 which read:

TO BE LET. An extensive and well established Fire Brick and Tile Works, situated at the Five Houses, Horwich Moor, the present proprietor being desirous of retiring from the business.
The works are complete with Steam Engine, Grinding and Crushing apparatus, Stoves, Drying Houses, Ovens, Moulds and every convenience for carrying out business.
The clay and coal being of superior quality, and are got on the premises at very trifle expense.
P.S. Any person taking the works can be accommodated with five or six acres of land and a few cottages adjoining.
For particulars apply to Mr Wm. Garbutt in the premises, or on Monday at the King's Arms and Four Horse Shoes Bolton.

I have been unable to source any photo of the Brick and Tile works so far - and I have not managed to find its date of closure or demolition. The tramway mentioned early, and visible on the photo, was used to carry the coal and clay from a mine level situated higher up the "valley" transporting these directly into the brick works. Little now remains of the works apart from a few walls and various mounds of rubble. It is however worth investigating the two "mounds" furthest away from the crash barrier, for these were obviously the site of the two kilns. The general design of the kilns can be clearly seen, along with some of the fused and once molten internal brickwork – caused due to the intense heat within the kilns. It would be interesting if someone could provide a plan of the works then we would all know what the various "mounds" around the site once were.

At one time there was, I understand, a cottage (illustrated above) near to the brickwork known as the "Hole Bottom Bungalow". The bungalow was latterly used as a Scout Hut until some point in the 1960's when it was demolished. The photo is merely a scan of a photocopy of the original photograph and I have no further information on the subject – although I presume this is a property which was marked as "Winter Hill House" on some maps produced around 1950.

Five Houses.

The earliest mention I can find of Five Houses is in connection with the 1838 murder of George Henderson (see an earlier article). Old maps indicate that this was a row of five houses as the name implies. One of these properties was used as an "ale house" and it was at this house that the murdered man, the travelling salesman George Henderson, used to meet his fellow salesman Benjamin Birrell every other Friday for a drink at 11.am. After Henderson was shot he was carried down to Five Houses where he was seen by a doctor but he later died. The alleged killer, a James Whittle, miner, also lived at Five Houses.

Looking at the 1881 Census it is noted that two families lived in the properties at that time:

Dwelling: Hole Bottom, Horwich Lancashire

	Marr	Age	Sex	Birthplace	Occupation
William Thompson M Terra Cotta works	M	45	M	Leeds(Rainow),York	Burner,
Ann Thompson	M	44	F	Rainow, Cheshire	Wife
Fred Thompson works	U	19	M	Rainow Cheshire	Terra Cotta
Samuel Thompson works	U	16	M	Rainow, Cheshire	Terra Cotta
Fanny Thompson		11	F	Rainow Cheshire	

Sarah A Thompson		9	F	Horwich, Lancs	Scholar
Frank Thompson		8	M	Horwich, Lancs	Scholar
Ada Thompson		6	F	Horwich, Lancs	Scholar
George Wilkinson		11months	M	Bolton, Lancs	Boarder

Dwelling : Hole Bottom, Horwich, Lancashire

Price Hampson	M	55	M	Flint, Wales	Terra Cotta Works
Harriet Hampson	M	54	F	Bolton, Lancs	Wife
James Hampson	U	26	M	Flint, Wales	Terra Cotta Works.

There is now nothing to see at the site of Five Houses.

The photo above shows all that is now left of the Hole Bottom Brickworks.

TWO LADS HILL.

In between Rivington Pike and the road to the TV mast lies a small hill with an obvious cairn on top of it. This is "Two Lads", or "Twa Lads" as it has sometimes been called in the past (or still seems to be called this by some with a strong local accent). There are several major routes used to get to the top of the hill, two from the TV mast road and the other starting next to Sportsman's Cottage on George's Lane.

There are many conflicting stories about the history of Two Lads and how it got its name. One tale has it that the cairn (an earlier one, not the present one) was built in remembrance of two boys who were lost in a snow storm some 400 years ago "their rigid bodies discovered frozen to each other in a final vain attempt for warmth". The other tale goes back a lot earlier to Saxon times (the name Rivington is believed to be of Saxon origin derived from "The Town of the Ravens") when there was some sort of encampment on Two Lads. It is said that the two sons of a local Saxon "king" had the monument built for the funeral of their father. As T Morris in the first issue of the "Rivington Review" pointed out, the latter theory for the name is quite credible, as Saxon funerals tended to be on higher ground where this was possible.

Just to confuse the issue, there is yet a third tradition of the story which has it that the two lads who perished in the snow were orphans of a Saxon King who was himself killed in battle. Another writer has suggested that the name Wilders Moor derives from the fact that the "two lads" became "wildered" (bewildered) or lost on the moor. *Gladys Sellers in her book "Walks on the West Pennine Moors" says that "Two Lads Moor" used to have two Bronze Age burial mounds close to the track and not far from the top. In fact they gave the moor its name. They were excavated long ago and no records of their contents were ever made. Not even their sites can be seen today"* Anyone any other theories to add? We'll never know the truth but what a fascinating story - whichever of them might be true.

Although I've never found a thing on Two Lads, despite 30 years of searching, I understand that Mr John Winstanley carried out some excavations (date unknown) on Two Lads and "discovered items of pottery, tools and human remains some of which date back to pre-historic times".

The present cairns on top of the hill are not the original ones. These were reputed to have been located in a slightly different spot but no remains of them now exist.

One of the main mining tunnels underneath Winter Hill passes almost directly underneath Two Lads (about 50 yards to the North to be exact – there is a photo elsewhere in this book of that tunnel)) heading from the field in front of Sportsman's Cottage almost to the TV mast. All the coal and clay from directly underneath Two Lads summit has been removed , half in 1919 and half in 1930. The surrounding areas of the hill were mined between approximately 1914 and 1957. There is also a small quarry on the south-western flank of the hill, a most odd spot for such an undertaking unless the stone were needed extremely locally, Hole Bottom perhaps, or even for any early "encampment" on the hill itself.

The hill is part encircled by a ditch. Some folk claim this was once part of the hills ancient defences, but others tell me this is a modern development, and is purely to do with water drainage. Still others say it's a mixture of the two.

In the late 80's there was a local "storm" in the Bolton Evening News both in articles and especially on the letters pages. Over the years the Two Lads cairn had virtually vanished and was in ruins. In 1988 a "mystery man" started to rebuild the cairn (I have since learned that the "mystery man" was David A Owen!). This task was then taken over by amateur historian Robin Smith who took over the task of restoring the monument to its original glory and he added a further four feet to the structure both by adding to it in height as well as clearing away rubble from the base.

During the digging he found the remains of old pots, jars, pieces of leather and clay smoking pipes he believed could date back one or two centuries. His most amazing discovery came when he dug to the bottom of the cairn and hit solid stone. He believed this could be the top of another ancient construction, adding weight to many historians view that the cairn marks the site of a Bronze or Iron Age fortress.

The council took offence at this "new" structure (especially its 10 foot height) and claimed it was dangerous and proceeded to pull it down! Undeterred, the mound was once again rebuilt by local people in 1989 but it was promptly pulled back down again by the authorities! Two Lads became known as "the Yo Yo cairn"!

One reason for the council pulling it down is a bit rich – it is too big! A sketch of Two Lads was drawn by Albison of Bolton 200 years ago which clearly showed that even in those days it was about eight feet high and thirteen feet in diameter!

Springs and Dingle Reservoirs

Although this book was only intended to cover the main area of Winter Hill, as the Springs and Dingle reservoirs take all their water from the north-eastern flanks of the hill, it was felt worthy of inclusion. The reservoirs lie next to the A657 on Belmont road between Bolton and Belmont. The two reservoirs lie next to each other with Dingle being a little lower and near to Bolton. Springs holds 134 million gallons and has a maximum depth of 48 feet whilst Dingle can contain 79 million gallons and is 30 feet deep. The total length of the embankments of both reservoirs is over three quarters of a mile in length, quite an undertaking for when they were constructed in the early 1800's.

Springs reservoir takes its name from the source of its water, from the springs on Daddy Meadows and was Bolton's first major reservoir supplying water to the town. Dingle reservoir takes its name from Shaly Dingle where the stream was diverted in order to supply the water to the new reservoir.

There was a problem that had to be overcome before both these reservoirs could be built. In nearby Eagley Brook, there were a number of water powered mills who derived a considerable amount of the water needed for their power from the flanks of Winter Hill. Before permission could be obtained to build the reservoirs, the Bolton Waterworks Company had to undertake to build a further large reservoir at Belmont (on the site of a much earlier smaller one) from which water would be released daily to compensate the mill owners for the loss of water from the Winter Hill Springs.

As well as Springs, Dingle and Belmont there is also a smaller reservoir in the area, Wards, usually known as the "Blue Lagoon". This was built in the early 19th century to supply water to Rycroft Works which was at the side of High Street on the spot now comprising the Brookdale Estate. The reservoir was enlarged in 1893 by Deacons who used the water to improve the water supplies to Belmont Bleachworks.

The major water supply for Springs reservoir comes from a man made well on Daddy Meadows. A friend once commented that at one time he had come across an old map which indicated that in this area there were "wind pumps". I have never seen a copy of this map. He went on to explain that in the 1960's he had a vague recollection of seeing old metal "mast type" structure (old USA style wind pump perhaps) in the area. Whilst looking through some photo's lent to me by to this person, I found the photograph shown below (I think it came from an old Bolton Waterworks publication). When checking on a 1947 Waterworks plan I note that "Springs Well" is the direct feed point for Springs reservoir – along with "Daddy Meadows Springs". The date of the photo is unknown.

SPRINGS WELL BORING PLANT

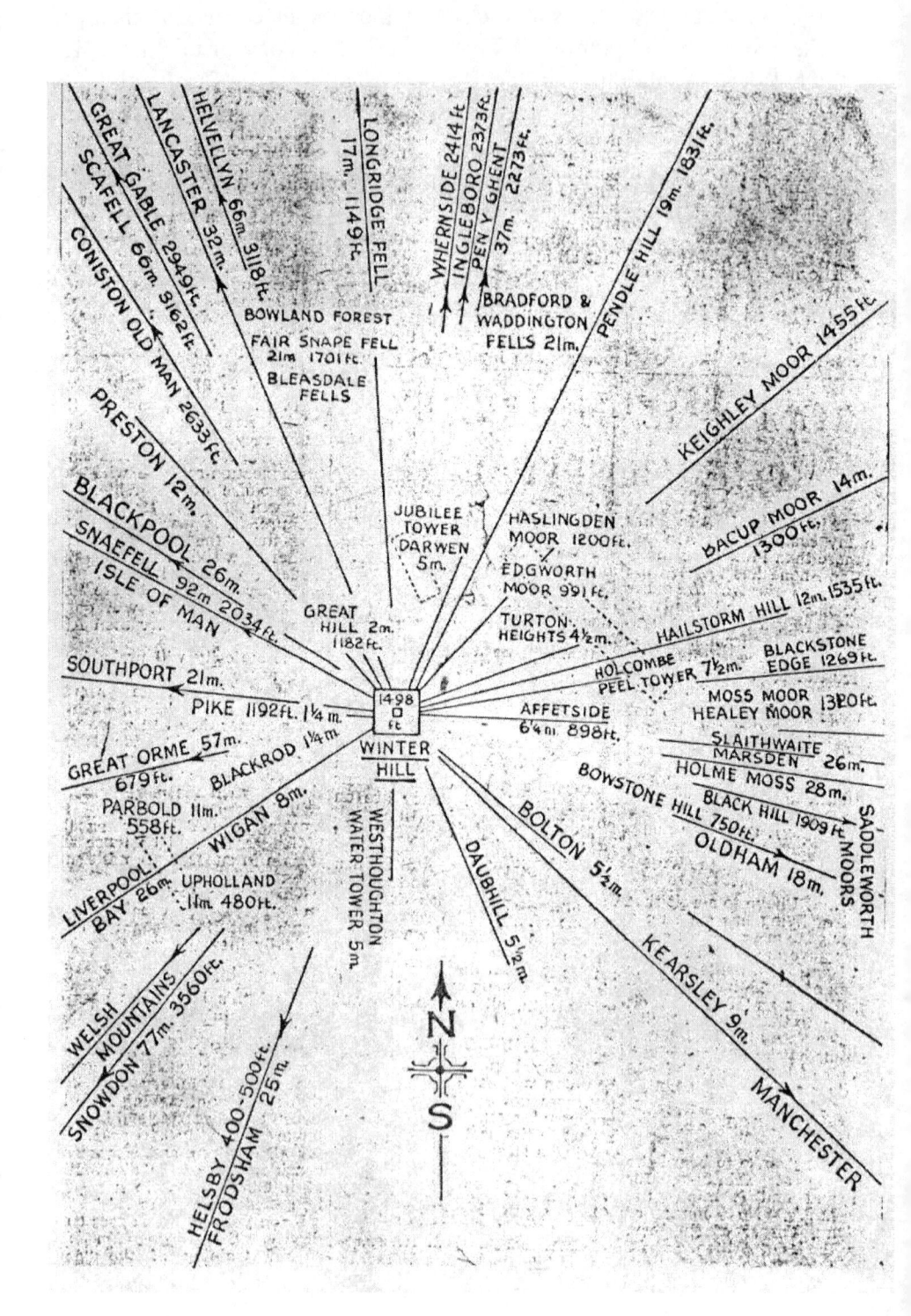

A panoramic direction diagram centred on **WINTER HILL (1498 ft)** showing bearings and distances to surrounding landmarks:

- GREAT GABLE 2949 ft
- SCAFELL 66m 3162 ft
- CONISTON OLD MAN 2633 ft
- LANCASTER 66m
- HELVELLYN 66m 3118 ft
- LONGRIDGE FELL 17m 1149 ft
- BOWLAND FOREST
- FAIR SNAPE FELL 21m 1701 ft
- BLEASDALE FELLS
- WHERNSIDE 2414 ft
- INGLEBORO 2373 ft
- PEN Y GHENT 37m 2273 ft
- BRADFORD & WADDINGTON FELLS 21m
- PENDLE HILL 19m 1831 ft
- KEIGHLEY MOOR 1455 ft
- PRESTON 12m
- BLACKPOOL 26m
- SNAEFELL 92m 2034 ft
- ISLE OF MAN
- JUBILEE TOWER DARWEN 5m
- HASLINGDEN MOOR 1200 ft
- EDGWORTH MOOR 991 ft
- BACUP MOOR 14m 1300 ft
- GREAT HILL 2m 1182 ft
- TURTON HEIGHTS 4½m
- HAILSTORM HILL 12m 1535 ft
- SOUTHPORT 21m
- HOLCOMBE PEEL TOWER 7½m
- BLACKSTONE EDGE 1269 ft
- PIKE 1192 ft 1¼m
- AFFETSIDE 6¼m 898 ft
- MOSS MOOR / HEALEY MOOR 1320 ft
- GREAT ORME 57m 679 ft
- BLACKROD 1¼m
- SLAITHWAITE MARSDEN 26m
- HOLME MOSS 28m
- PARBOLD 11m 558 ft
- WIGAN 8m
- BOWSTONE HILL 750 ft
- BLACK HILL 1909 ft
- SADDLEWORTH MOORS
- LIVERPOOL BAY 26m
- UPHOLLAND 11m 480 ft
- WESTHOUGHTON WATER TOWER 5m
- BOLTON 5½m
- OLDHAM 18m
- WELSH MOUNTAINS
- DAUBHILL 5½m
- KEARSLEY 9m
- SNOWDON 77m 3560 ft
- HELSBY 400–500 ft
- FRODSHAM 25m
- MANCHESTER

N / S compass rose at bottom.

More Winter Hill Mining Remains.

Since writing volume 1 of this book, I have received many enquiries about the coal mine's and tunnels under Winter Hill. A large number of people have asked "Are there any other mining remains other than the things you have written about". A very difficult question to answer! As explained earlier, it would be foolish to fully describe ALL details of mines under Winter Hill because this would merely encourage every adventurous minded person in the area to descend on them and to explore them. I am however tempted to give details of a few other finds in the area just to educate people as to what is there. So here goes. I'll give a few more brief descriptions of other interesting things to see – but please don't pester me via email for any EXACT details other than what is written below. All workings mentioned below are either fully sealed up, have a blockage near to the entrance (rockfall, roof collapse etc) or have been filled in by the explorers after finding nothing of interest.

Another "Montcliffe area" mine.

Apart from the main Montcliffe Mine and the associated Margery Drift, there is another rather odd mine in the same general area. Entrance to this mine was effected by squeezing through a small hole at the top of a wall and for this reason (and because it was VERY wet) I declined to enter and so my description is merely what I have been told. I nearly always decline to physically explore tunnels these days!

Dropping through the hole you enter a concrete roofed flooded area with man made stone walls and after a few yards there is a passage on the right hand side, the tunnel straight ahead being chest deep in water. The RH tunnel goes nowhere. Following the main tunnel, the water shallows and eventually becomes reasonably dry underfoot.

I am told that parts of this mine are somewhat "cave like" with a running stream in one section which heads off downhill.

Wilderswood area.

There are at least two old tunnels in this area which can be clearly seen by any passing walker so I am giving away no secrets. Both are a waste of time exploring internally for they are both totally blocked after a few yards with major roof falls – and I mean "major"!

Taking the path from Ormston's farm (from the bottom of Ormston Lane) that heads towards the bottom end of Wilderswood, you pass over a bridge spanning the stream. Look over the upstream parapet and on the right hand bank you will be able to see the entrance to a small tunnel. This is blocked only a few yards in and any attempt to excavate would probably collapse the roadway that passes over it. Nothing is known about this tunnel and I have seen no maps or charts relating to any underground workings under Wilderswood.

Carry on up the path and after 100 yards or so, pass through the hole in the right hand wall (where a "cabin" once stood, reputedly to record the amounts of coal coming out of the local workings) and go up the steps to the footpath. After a few yards drop down to stream level and head upstream and soon you will find another tunnel entrance. This one is strange and nobody has so far been able to explain its purpose. The size of the tunnel indicates a fairly major mine entrance, but in order to enter it, you first of all have to drop down into a sort of well about 3 feet deep. Whether this "well" is a later development is not known, but for this to be any sort of working mine entrance, there should not be a well or wall there which would have prevented any easy coal extraction from the mine. Yet another of this areas mysteries! This tunnel is also blocked after a few yards and the site of the collapse can be seen from the banking higher up the slope.

There are other suspected mine workings in the area but all are either totally sealed, collapsed, or can no longer be found despite being marked on early maps. In a later volume I'll try to get round to giving a step by step guide to this general area so to make a visit here more interesting.

A bricked up adit entrance at Hole Bottom

Winter Hill & Noon Hill Burial Mounds.

(The following is an article was written by J Rawlinson and published in the Chorley & District Archaeological Society Bulletin Sept & Dec 1961. It describes the discovery and excavation of the Winter Hill Barrow.) The barrow is marked on modern maps as "Tumulus" or "Cairn".

In the district of Central Lancashire there are several authentic burial mounds. On Anglezarke Moors there is a large round barrow called "Round Loaf". It is possible this covers a stone chambered grave. On the same moor there is a site called Pike Stones, a ruined chambered grave from which the farmers have taken a lot of stone. Both these are marked on the OS maps.

On Rivington Moor there is a saucer tumulus called "Noon Hill", famous locally for more than 400 years, and Winter Hill Round Barrow which was discovered by Mr Tom Creear and myself in March 1957.

On Horwich Moor, there is "Two Lads", a site encircled by earthworks, which once contained two stone cairns surrounded by a stone wall with an entrance from the east. Nearer Bolton just outside the Horwich boundary is a barrow with the interesting name of "Priests Crown". This mound and Two Lads are marked on the OS map.

To return to the Winter Hill Round Barrow. On Sunday afternoon 24th March 1957, whilst searching for a possible Roman signalling and observation station on Winter Hill, Mr Creear and I discovered a curved line of stones about 20 feet long just peeping out of the turf. Investigation proved these to be part of a stone circle about 63 feet in diameter. Inside the circle there was a pile of stones forming an inner circle with a slight depression in the centre. The site commanded a wonderful view of Lancashire and its surroundings, only a small section of about 30 degrees to the South of East being obscured by the hills. Just north of east the southern slopes of Pendle Hill were to be seen with the way into Yorkshire through Burnley and Colne. West of Pendle, on a clear day, Ingleborough, Penygent and Whernside come into view. Continuing West, Longridge and Bleasedale Fells can be followed bringing the sea coast into view near Pilling. The coast is visible to Great Ormes Head at Llandudno in North Wales including the estuaries of the Ribble and the Mersey and in an arc from SW to SE the view continues to the Peak District of Derbyshire .... Including the industrial sprawl around Warrington and Manchester, and occasionally above all Snowdon and the Carnedds peep out of the clouds.

On Friday evening 21st June 1957 I took Mr Rosser to the Winter Hill Barrow site and he was very impressed. Mr Creear and myself revisited the site on 29th June. Mr Creear exposed about 30 feet of the outer wall whilst I dug a trial hole in the west side of the circle, here I found the wall 25 inches high resting on the cleared surface of the moor. I took two photos, one from the west and two from the south-west before starting work on the site. This work was reported at the Society meeting on July 4th and another visit arranged for Saturday July 6th to expose more of the outside wall. Nineteen members of the Society visited the site as arranged and about fifty feet of the outer wall was exposed, the work was then stopped and we reported the situation to Mr Rosser. On Tuesday 6th August Professor A Whallet, Dr Bulock and Mr C EP Rosser visited the site and stated that it was a Bronze Age Barrow and would be scheduled by the Ministry of Works. Later it was decided to excavate the barrow the following summer. On Friday afternoon the 18th July 1958 together with Mr Ron Rigby, our Society Vice Chairman, I met Dr Bullock and Mr C E P Rosser on the site on Winter Hill. We pegged out the south-west section and arranged for work to commence on the following Monday the 21st. I also arranged for hot lunches to be delivered on the site for the week from Rivington Hall Barn.

On Monday and Tuesday the excavation went steadily on without any outstanding incident. The pattern formed on the vertical face of the excavation was very interesting, the mixture of clay about four different colours from cream to brown with the network effect of the turf lines produced a design almost like a continental cheese. This basket filling continued all the way through the mound but about halfway to the centre there was a plainer sloping turf line as though the centre cairn had been covered first and the space left to the outer wall filled in later.

On Wednesday afternoon a flurry of excitement was caused by the discovery of a squarely cut piece of wood (birch) lying on the last layer of turf at a depth of 3 feet from the surface and 13 feet from the centre of the mound. The wood was very soft and wet and to prevent it drying out and crumbling after measuring, it was covered with a wet sack. The stick was 2 foot 2 inches long by 2 inches wide and almost one inch thick. I suggested to Mr Rosser that perhaps it had been used as a measuring stick. Later two samples about 3 inches long were taken for tests. I was promised one of these at some future date with a report.

On reaching the centre portion we found a large quantity of stone which had been a central cairn and a thick almost vertical turf line which led one to believe that the centre had been disturbed. Dr Bullock said this was probably about 200 years ago. Another section of the north east of the mound was commenced and later two square holes 6 ft by 6 ft near the centre were dug. Nothing more was found but the two professionals said that they were perfectly satisfied with the excavation which had proved that the site was a burial mound and the stick of wood would eventually give its age. Personally, I was disappointed I thought that the whole mound should have been excavated. The following month, August, the newly formed Bolton Archaeological Society under the leadership of Mr J Winstanly commenced to excavate Noon Hill, Rivington, in the Chorley Rural Area and about three-quarters of a mile from the Winter Hill Mound.

We had photographed and measured Noon Hill two years ago and I had taken Dr Bullock and a small party there whilst we were working on Winter Hill. Dr Bullock gave the opinion that it had been dug. I visited Noon Hill on the Wednesday of the second week of the excavation and found a south-eastern quadrant excavated to the inner wall. In the south-eastern quadrant the inner wall had been completely taken out and evidence of three burial found there. One had a shattered urn but only a small heap of burnt bones were found to mark the other two.

Two tanged and barbed flint arrowheads were unearthed and a small flint knife blade with one edge fine toothed like a saw and the other a straight sharpened edge. All probably votive from the burials. The bones had apparently been broken up to go into the urns, and some of these were later found to be a child's. The shattered urn of a dirty yellow colour has now been rebuilt and is on exhibition at Bolton *Museum (it is now no longer exhibited but is held in the museum storage area).* The excavation showed an outer circle formed of a double ring of large stones, this circle is about 52 feet in diameter, an inner wall of smaller stones, mostly boulders, was strengthened by several buttress stones. The wall is three feet high and forms a ring 33 feet in diameter, the burials were found built into this wall.

The filling of this mound was much darker than that on Winter Hill, more loam and less clay so the turf lines were not so plain. The urn is 10 inches in height, 9 inches in largest diameter, base 4 inches diameter and a simple design of straight lines covers the top half. The excavation was stopped soon after my visit to be resumed next summer under C.B.A. direction.

Two Lads is a hill 1275 feet above sea level and almost a mile south east from Rivington Pike. On the summit is a large pile of stones and between the summit and the 1150 feet contour there are 1 mile & 1500 yards of earthworks. In places these have been altered and adapted for water conservancy purposes but sufficient can be seen to lead one to believe that they constituted a breastwork and trench system of defences. The cairn on the summit has been built from two cairns, and a surrounding wall around the year 1800 by a local lord of the manor so that it could be discerned from his residence. The famous antiquary Durning Rasbotham visited this hill in 1776 and our reconstruction is from his description. The hill has been a prolific source of flint finds for a long time. I cannot find any mention of an excavation here but I hope to take a Yorkshire Archaeologist who has had experience on Pennine Sites over the hill.

John Rawlinson.
Chorley and District Archaeological Society Bulletin.

An unexplained mystery.

Since the writing of Volume 1 of this scrapbook, I have received a number of e-mails from various people around the world who have all added a little bit to my knowledge of Winter Hill. One such person lived for a period at Sportsman's Cottage in the mid 1950's and I repeat below exactly what that person wrote because not only is it a fascinating story, but I also wonder if anyone has had any other "strange" experiences either on Winter Hill or on the nearby moors. Any similar information received will be most welcome for us all to share (e-mail me at d.lane@btinternet.com).

"I would like to tell you something that happened on the moors one night. My Grandad was a no-nonsense man who had been a policeman in Liverpool for many years before his retirement to Rivington. He was not a fanciful man nor a liar. I was staying with them , as usual, and when I got up this particular morning I knew something was wrong....my Nan packed my stuff and some for her and Grandad and took me home to Liverpool.......they never went back to Rivington, to Sportsmans Cottage !! It was not until many years later that I found out what made them abandon their home overnight.

My Grandad had got up in the night to use the toilet and, as you would, had looked out of the window over the black moors. He saw something out on the moors that made him tell my Nan he wouldn't spend another night there and they came to stay with us until they could find somewhere to live. They never went back there to stay, only to pack up and move out.

My Grandad would never tell anyone what he saw, not even my Nan, and the secret died with him. All I know is that it scared him to death and made him move out straight away. I missed Rivington a lot. Do you know of anything that my Grandad could have seen? Are there any tales of strange things up there? I have wondered about it all my life and if anyone else has ever seen anything that affected them" .

Can you add anything to this recollection? Have you experienced anything similar?

Another "ghostly" occurrence in the vicinity.

Although not strictly on Winter Hill, Anderton is near enough to the base of the hill to include the following snippets! They are taken from the Bolton Evening News dated December 4th 1982 and from a letter written in the same newspaper on Thursday the 23rd December 1982.

Pub's spirit gives staff the shakes. *Licensee Mr Richard Calvert reckons there are more spirits in his pub than behind the bar. A catalogue of strange sightings and weird experiences by members of staff at the Millstone Hotel, Anderton, near Horwich, over three years has convinced Mr Calvert that a "grey lady" exists. The latest incident centred on the coffee lounge. Mr Calvert said "We showed a couple in there and asked them to sit near the fireplace. Almost immediately the woman came out shaking, saying there was a ghost. She was gasping for breath and trembling".*

But most reports of mysterious presence at the Millstone focus on the main restaurant, known as "the back room". Mrs Lynne Edwards, of Mary Street East, Horwich, worked at the Millstone as a cleaner for two years. She said "The first time I saw something strange was one morning when we had all been sitting in the bar area having our coffee break. I felt a strange sensation that there was someone watching me from the back restaurant. I glanced up and saw this grey outline."

Mother of two, Mrs Janice Tyrer of Wright Street, Horwich, confesses to be "terrified" of being alone in the back room. She has worked as a cleaner at the Millstone for the past four years. Mr Calvert spoke of other strange happenings at the pub, like the burglar alarm going off in the middle of the night. He said that the previous licensee had an alsatian, which refused to go in the back room and in an upstairs bedroom. One of the questions now being asked is could the Millstone Phantom be the Phantom of Headless Cross?

Headless Cross is 200 yards from the pub and there have been many reports of a monk crossing the road. The sightings are based on an age-old story about Father Bennett who was head of Lady Chapel –

now covered by Lower Rivington reservoir. During the Reformation Father Bennett, fearing that valuables in the chapel would be plundered, decided to hide them. He entered a tunnel that was supposed to lead to the chapel and was never seen again.

The latest reports of ghostly goings-on centre on Headless Cross House. Mr Anthony Samuels and his family live there. Mr Samuel's runs a business in St George's Road, Bolton, said they returned from their summer holidays last year to find all the lights on. Yet there was no shred of evidence of any intruders. He said: "Every so often, my wife can see a face on the door of the bedroom wardrobe".

++

Was it the "ghost" of priest daughter said. Sir ...I was very interested to read your report of the ghost of the "grey lady" seen in and around the Millstone at Anderton, Lancs.

My daughter Tracy, who was then eight, saw her in May 1978. The "lady" was standing in the centre of a small stone hump backed bridge in Grimeford Lane, leading from near the Millstone to the A6 at Blackrod. We had been to the Millstone with my parents and two children and were taking my parent's home to Blackrod at the time she was sighted. It was about 10 o'clock on a lovely summer night as we were driving down the Lane.

As we approached the bridge Tracy saw a lady dressed in a long grey dress, a cape and with something on her head, which she could not describe properly at the time, standing as if waiting to cross the road. As we drove past her she suddenly disappeared. You should have heard Tracy's reaction when this happened. She just could not believe it as she thought she had seen a real live person.

No one else in the car saw her except Tracy insisted she was there and started to describe her in great detail. At this a cold shiver ran down my spine as I remembered my parents telling me of a ghost that used to haunt the lane when I was a child. She said she was rather tall and seemed old but she did not see her features clearly. She also wanted to know what a lady was doing down a lonely lane on her *own at that time of night. She said that the dress was so long that "I thought she'd been to a party".*

■■

Later I started to draw pictures of what she said she had seen and, after drawing lots of different headwear, the thing she wore on her head turned out to be a barreta, the small four cornered cap that priests wear. Tracey has maintained all along that what she saw was a lady but when the Pope visited Britain in May and she saw a full length shot of him on television she said "that lady" was wearing exactly the same clothes but they were grey.

Last year we got a book from the library about Rivington and the story of Father Bennett was in it. We think this is what Tracy saw as he used to travel round from village to village blessing the people. We were also told by someone that priests around those times used to stand at the crossing of a ford and bless the travellers as they went by. The bridge where Tracy saw the ghost was across a small stream which probably many years ago could have been the crossing of a ford.

I hope this letter sheds a little more light on the mystery as it certainly gives us food for thought knowing that someone else has seen the "grey lady" besides our daughter... Mrs Brenda Smith, Horwich.

Horwich Journal 23rd December 1927. Yet another ghostly occurrence!

An account of a ghost story – 25 years ago Mr and Mrs W H Lever were returning from Chorley to their bungalow in a coach and horses when, on the steepest part of the old road leading up from Lower House Farm to the Pigeon Tower, the two horses stopped and refused to go any further. Mr and Mrs Lever had to walk the rest of the way.

The horses and carriage were turned with great difficulty and taken home another way. Both the coachman and servants averred that the road was haunted and would not travel the road again after dark.

Aeroplane Crashes on and around Winter Hill

There have been a remarkably large number of plane crashes either on Winter Hill itself or in the surrounding area. Various people have compiled lists of these crashes and more information has come to light following articles in the Bolton Evening News. Unfortunately I can't give credit to the people who have provided this information for all I have are unsigned sheets of paper with the information on them. Below is a list of the crashes I am aware of:

Date	Type	Location	Remarks
1915		Bob's Brow, Horwich	Single seat fighter RFC
Apr-20		Nr Nab Gate Harwood Ramsden's Meadows	Sir Alan Cobham & passenger unhurt
7.28	Atlas biplane	Winter Hill/Belmont Riv Rd	FO Walker. From Sealand to Catterick
3.4.29	DH Moth	Markland Hill Lane	R Taggert
15.11.35	Puss Moth	Crowthorne Hill	Lancashire Aero Club
6.6.36	DH Rapide	Nr Dean Golf Club	Pilots & passengers unhurt. IOM to Barton
37	Moth type?	Crowthorne Moor	Mail plane. IOM to Mc/r
17.8.37		No 50 Mornington Rd	Sgt Blackburn killed
		Little Hulton	RAF plane force landed
38/39	Roc	Stocks Park, Horwich	
13.2.41	Spitfire	Ashton Field, Little Hulton	Pilot had severe facial injuries
5.41	Skua	Golf Course Horwich	Fleet Air Arm
1.9.42	P 38	Sowall Farm, Westhoughton	Williams
7.8.42	Argus	Winter Hill. North side	5 ADG. 5 occupants uninjured
3.2.43	Skua	Dunscar	776 Squadron, RNAS, Stretton to Speke

Date	Aircraft	Location	Notes
16.11.43	Wellington	Lodge Hurst Hill, Anglezarke	28 OTU. All crew killed
24.12.43	Oxford	Winter Hill	410 Squadron RAF
13.1.44	B 7G	Crowthorne Hill	
44		Bryan Hey Reservoir	On flight to Burtonwood
2.2.45	Hurricane	Horrocks Field Farm, Scout Rd	N T Huddle Flt Sgt killed
2.2.45	Hurricane	Whimberry Hill	P S Taylor Flt Sgt killed
29.7.45	Mustang 3	Cadshaw Bridge/Bull Hill	W O Hoga Polish Squadron 12 Group killed
1946	Spitfire	Darwen Moor	
14.9.53	Meteor	Crowthorne Hill	2 planes crashed. 610 Squadron. Hooton Park
27.2.58	Bristol 170	Winter Hill	35 died, 7 survived
22.12.65	Chipmunk	Smithills Moor	Manchester UAS flying from Woodvale
8.68	Cessna 172	Winter Hill	Pilot survived, Pleasure flight Blackpool, to Barton
29.9.77	Horizon	Whittle Pike, Scout Moor	2 killed, Yeadon to Barton
21.1.78	Piper TriPacer	Georges Lane, Horwich	3 killed. Flew into wall in rain & mist
Circa 1944	Spitfire	Nr Bay Horse, Heath Charnock	One cow killed!

The most disastrous crash on Winter Hill occurred on the 27th February 1958 when a Bristol Wayfarer of Silver City Airlines crashed on the summit of Winter Hill with 35 people losing their lives. The aircraft had left Ronaldsway on the Isle of Man with a party of motor traders on board who were on their way to the Exide Battery Works at Clifton Junction. It was mid morning when the crash occurred following a navigation error.

When the Silver City Airlines plane took off from Ronaldsway all was in order. Charlie Sierra, flew over the Irish Sea at 1,500 feet, with the crew expecting a lift in altitude when they reached the

Lancashire coast. It never came and Captain Edward Cairns was asked if he could maintain the same height by Air Traffic Control at Preston. He agreed, and was told by his First Officer William Howarth that the planes radar compass was tuned to the beacon at Wigan. What the crew did not realise was that through an elementary mistake they had picked up the wrong beacon call sign. Instead of being on course for Wigan – call sign MYK, the ill-fated plane was heading for MYL – the Oldham beacon.

Watching the radar screen at Ringway Airport was zone controller Maurice Ladd. It was 9.44am when he picked up a faint radar signal to pinpoint Charlie Sierra somewhere over Chorley. Immediately Mr Ladd gave the order that Charlie Sierra should turn right on to a course of 250 degrees. Despite his split second decision, it was too late. The Wayfarer, already heading straight for the range of hills – and with the odds-against chance of flying "blind" through a gap in them – altered course. Unfortunately, through no-one's fault, the advice came vital seconds too late. The plane, by now in the cloud, veered to the right, but instead of open airspace her two-man crew were confronted by the bleak rearing hillside.

A total of 35 people lost their lives in the crash and there were seven survivors including the crew. The planes First Officer staggered the 350 yards from the scene of the crash to the Winter Hill ITA transmitter to raise the alarm. The aircraft had broken into three pieces, with only the tail recognisable as part of a plane

Conditions on the hill were appalling and rescuers had to struggle through snow sometimes six feet deep to get to the crash. Fog brought visibility down to almost zero and although ambulances were sent from nearly every nearby town they were held up until a bulldozer had cleared a path for them. Three RAF helicopters were sent to the scene, one with a doctor on board but fog prevented them from landing. The survivors were taken to Bolton Royal Infirmary.

There is now a plaque commemorating the crash mounted on the side of the TV station and is visible from the road.

The commemorative plaque on the wall of the TV station.

Newspaper photo of the RAF Chipmunk that crashed on Smithills Moor in December 1965

Access to the Moors.

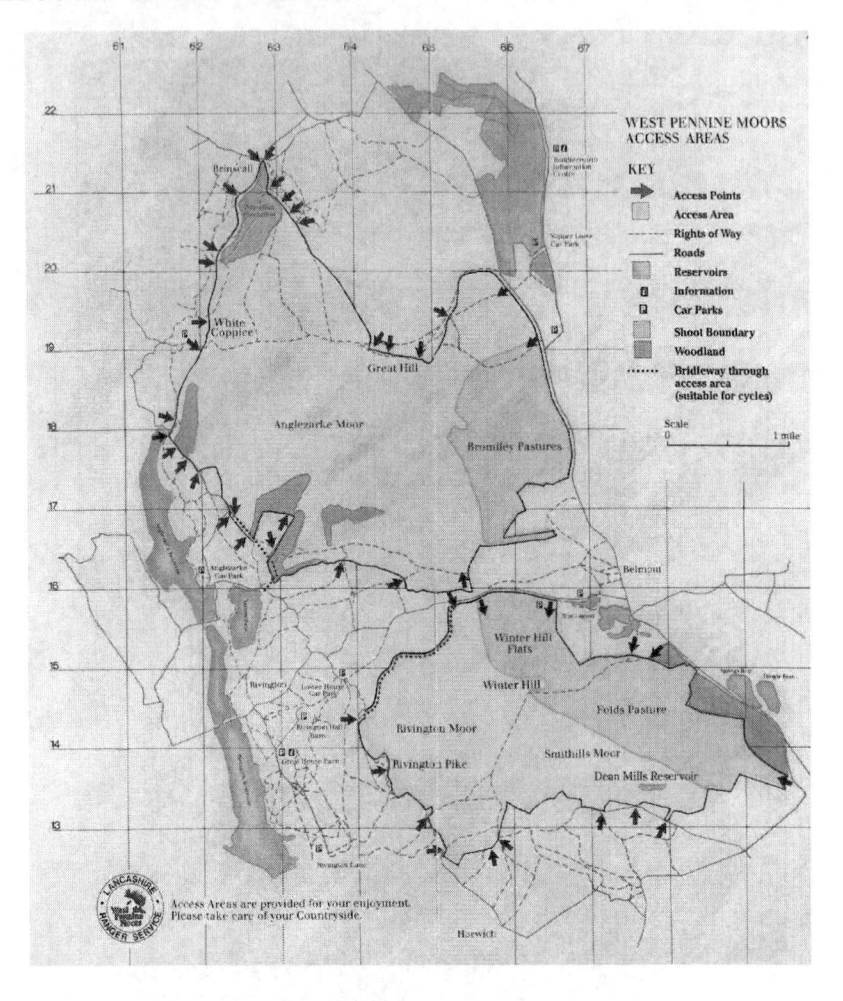

All of the land is owned by "someone". Winter Hill and the surrounding areas are all owned by somebody whether this be a private landlord, a water authority or a local authority. Although large areas of Winter Hill, Anglezarke Moor etc are open to the public there has to be some control over access to these areas so "access agreements" have been drawn up with all the local landlords involved. Apart from all the usual "rules" regarding how one should behave on the moors, there are clearly defined "access" points to get on to the moors (i.e. no climbing over walls, no crossing farmers fields etc in order to get onto the moors). The official map of all officially agreed access points is shown above ....
PLEASE STICK TO THEM AND RESPECT THEM!

RIVINGTON BUNGALOW TO GO
House and Gardens Everyone will Miss

FUTURE generations of Bolton folk, enjoying the splendid heritage of Lever Park, made theirs by the generosity of the first Lord Leverhulme, will probably look with puzzled eyes at the wooded slope of Rivington.

They will recall that the generous donor of an industrially-romantic day had a residence perched eyrie-like atop that hill. They will muse: "It has completely disappeared—pity!"

From the point of view of the lover of unusual things whether in houses and gardens, or jewels and music, it is a pity. But it seems inevitable. Liverpool Corporation have all along placed the unquestionable purity of the water collected on their great and beautiful gathering ground before the things of the spirit. And they, the last owners of The Bungalow, have this week signalized the last chapter of the strange story by proposing to hand the place, lock, stock, and barrel, as the saying is, to a demolition gang.

Soon then it will be gone, with all its striking characteristics that reflected the taste of its builder, and the hillside will return to the whispering solitudes, the wind, the rain, and the cry of the curlew.

Beautiful Tapestries

There was formerly at the Bungalow a collection of characteristic things—Lord Leverhulme's own almost monkish apartment, open mostly to the winds of heaven; his collection of beautiful tapestries in the hall, an attractive library of books beloved—almost a Lancashire anthology—and furniture worthy of a connoisseur; electric horses to take the place of flesh and blood mounts when years began to tell upon the busy Viscount.

He loved dancing, and it is no surprise to learn that he had a circular ballroom built whose perfect proportions and polished floor have delighted thousands of those to whom he so frequently threw open his house and grounds.

There was another feature that those who knew him understood. Although he was no great astrologer or astronomer he had his dining-room ceiling illuminated with the stars and planets as they were in their courses at the moment of his birth.

After his personal treasures no feature of the estate could so well reflect the man as the perfectly-proportioned gardens, green lawns and a miniature lake on levels carved out of the rock, waterfalls tumbling down the tree-clothed hillside, nooks and crannies filled with choice plants. And the Japanese gardens. These were planned in princely style. They were a romance of the landscape art, and nothing pleased their owner so much as to know his personal friends and his fellow townsmen of his beloved Bolton were enjoying them with him.

The Bungalow story is inseparable from that of his purchase in 1899 of the Rivington Hall estate from the agents of Mr. J. W. Crompton, of Rivington Hall.

He was living at Hillside, Heaton, at the time and as his son, the present Viscount, recalls in his memoirs, the proposal appealed to him. At Rivington he could make a "garden" in which his imagination could have full play.

"The rest of the estate he could offer to his native town as a park and so ensure the preservation of its beauties for the public, for Rivington Pike, some 1,200ft. above sea-level and one of the highest landmarks in this part of Lancashire had long been a favourite resort of the people of Bolton and the surrounding towns."

He fully realized the position and responsibility of the Liverpool Corporation Waterworks Committee, and it is noteworthy that at every stage he offered them first choice before he purchased the estate to fulfil his less utilitarian dreams.

Refused to Make Profit

And when Parliament decided in his favour and a commission fixed generous terms, he scrupulously refused to make a profit, devoting the surplus to Liverpool charity and to broadening the basis of the work of the Liverpool University, particularly in the study of architecture and civic design.

This bungalow scheme began as it has ended, on an unusual note. The first building was a bungalow of wood of simple design. This was replaced by a rather more elaborate residence—the one which it has since been admitted was burnt to the ground early in the morning of July 8th, 1913, by women suffrage extremists.

Then the Viscount built one, chiefly of local stone. One which he said could not be burnt down. Its terraces, garden houses and picturesque dove cotes we know. And in 1905 he started his garden scheme to plans drawn by Mr. Mawson, the eminent architect of Beautiful Bolton fame.

It is said that £250,000 was spent on the making of this attractive property.

After his death in 1925 the Bungalow and gardens were acquired by the late Mr. John Magee who, like Lord Leverhulme, welcomed visits of the public.

When Mr. Magee died, the property was placed on the market and conferences of representatives of local authorities and the Council for the Preservation of Rural England suggested that it would be acquired for the benefit of the public.

Negotiations were still proceeding when the Bolton Corporation Parks Committee surprisingly announced their retirement from the entire business, and whilst the Liverpool authority expressed sympathy with the project they did not give it any favour.

The war came so the remaining local authorities could not obtain a financial backing from the Government, and after unsuccessful efforts to defer the sale, the property went to the Liverpool Corporation at a cost, it is said, of £3,000.

To-day they are inviting offers for its demolition. Soon it will be gone. But the things it stood for, the love and preservation of the beauty that is so essentially ours, must not disappear with it.

BOLTON EVENING NEWS.
30TH MAY 1947.

The Natural Dangers of Winter Hill

All high moorland should be treated with respect, and Winter Hill is no exception. Whilst researching material for this scrapbook, I have come across numerous references of people who have had their lives at risk purely because they were "there". The bulk of the cases involve broken or twisted limbs or joints but a large number are due mainly to either the extreme weather or the pure physical conditions which exist at times and in certain places on the Hill.

There are reports of groups of youngster's entering old mines and getting lost – this was one of the prime reasons why mine shafts and collapsed entrances on Winter Hill are immediately filled in and sealed when they occur. People always refer to the day "those youngsters got lost down the tunnels"! It really happened!

There have been a number of cases of exposure on Winter Hill when ill-dressed folk have headed for the Hill in atrocious conditions. The weather in winter on Winter Hill can, on occasions, be just as extreme as one finds in the Scottish Mountains. I well remember one day on duty as a Ranger years ago in the Pigeon Tower/Rivington Pike area. A thin layer of snow had fallen the previous day, which had frozen solid overnight. A gale was blowing and ice particles were being ripped from the ground and blown in the air. To look around in any safety one had to wear goggles. The weather deteriorated and heavy snow fell, soon reaching the top of fence posts in places. At 4pm just as night was falling a call went out. Cries for help had been heard from the Pike. The weather conditions going up to the Pike were appalling with a snow blizzard obscuring all visibility – especially when carrying a stretcher! I forget exactly who was rescued or brought down that day but I write this just to illustrate how unforgiving Winter Hill can be at times. When I arrived home in Swinton that evening my wife looked uncomprehendingly at me as I explained my day …… as we had not had ANY snow in Swinton since the previous year! I'm sure she didn't believe a word I was saying! Winter Hill seemed a million miles away.

It is not always the weather or broken bones that can cause problems. In some isolated parts of the Hill the ground underfoot is not always as it seems! There are boggy areas and many people who love to get away from the recognised tracks have tales to tell …. me included! I am not referring to merely getting feet wet in a bog. Frequently one can go in up to the thighs. An article in the Bolton Evening News on Monday January 5th 1987 illustrates the dangers:

***Moor ordeal man thanks rescuers**. A walker who cheated death by an hour after a "quicksand" ordeal on a bleak moorland has thanked police for saving his life. Mr John Gill, aged 27, was found unconscious, 1,500 feet up on the access road to the TV mast on Winter Hill. He collapsed exhausted after struggling for two hours to free himself after falling into a ditch in the hill's peat bogs. The alarm was raised when a CB radio user spotted what he thought was a body on the tarmac road. Police searched by torchlight in a gale before finding Mr Gill, who lives at Ridgeway, Blackrod.*

Speaking for the first time about his ordeal Mr Gill said "I would like to thank the teenager who saw me and the police. I apologise for any trouble I have caused. I was up to my waist in the bog and was stuck completely. I struggled for hours to get out. I shouted for help but it was useless at that time of night and in a gale. When I got out of the bog by pulling at tufts of grass, I was exhausted and could not feel my hands or feet. I thought I was going to die. The bog was like quicksand – I was sinking fast the more I struggled"

Mr Gill, set out for a walk at 8.45pm but was found close to death nearly five hours later. He said "I remember the police finding me and the next thing I woke up in hospital and was being brought round with tea and an injection. I had suffered severe hypothermia"

Although Winter Hill is a wonderful "playground" and a place of great beauty and fascination for many of us, we should always be aware of the hidden dangers at all times, and do all we can to minimise them. Unfortunately, many of us like the bleakness and solitude of the place, and often go wandering around on our own - and at times when there is perhaps nobody else around on the moors – and in the most appalling weather conditions! Some would call us foolhardy, but this is our choice and what we choose to do - and we would defend our right to do just this – so long as we are all aware of the possible dangers and we dress and equip ourselves to minimise the risks.

In poor weather never underestimate Winter Hill. The bogs really ARE there. The visibility really CAN vanish totally within 60 seconds. The body surface temperature plus the chill factor for those unsuitably dressed, really CAN drop to −10C or more on top of the Hill.

DO take care on Winter Hill ..... but enjoy it! Remember. It CAN bite!

Liverpool Castle by the side of the Lower Rivington Reservoir. Photo taken from a rather low flying microlight piloted by the author of course!!!!

A photo taken in the 1940s or 1950's showing a tank lying alongside the Belmont to Rivington Road. People used to take their children to the moors ""to see the tank", which had been used as target practice during the late war.

The "building" of Scotsmans Stump circa 1912. (Photo copyright of Paul Lacey).

Winter Hill. A magnet for all UFO spotters!!

One of Winter Hill's claim to fame is that a remarkably large number of people claim to have spotted UFO's in its vicinity. The 1950's 60's and 70's local newspapers often commented on the latest "sightings". At times it seems to be getting very busy with UFO's in the area and in 1988 a local "ufologist" said that "over the past 5 years I have had about 100 calls about the Belmont area. When you think that many people are embarrassed or afraid to admit seeing UFO's, the number of sightings could be in the thousands". He went on to say "there is a concentration of sightings in Belmont and Horwich especially around the reservoirs. One theory is that they could be taking on water".

This photo is perhaps one of the most famous of all the "sightings" as it was taken in 1996 by a professional photographer who spotted the

UFO over Rivington!

Mysterious sighting over Bolton to be placed among the real 'X Files'

IAN SKELLY
BOLTON
FOR QUALITY NEW AND USED CARS
St. Georges Road, Bolton

"object" after he had his slide's developed! He passed the information over to the "Direct Investigation Group on Aerial Phenomena (DIGAP) who were convinced that British Aerospace at Wharton were developing a secret craft.

Another UFO "incident" occurred on the hill in 1999 which has been widely publicised on the Internet:

(http://www.maxpages.com/mapit/THE_WINTER_HILL_MIB_CASE). The excellent Winter Hill website at: http://www.winterhill.org/ufos.htm carries an article on the 1999 subject which describes the claims better than I could ever do and is reproduced below.

Thanks to Stephen Mera of "MAPIT" for his help in compiling this page.

The case of the "Winter Hill MIB UFO" sighting is one of the great mysteries of Winter Hill. In 1999, a farm worker by the name of Murphy spotted a strange object hanging over his cattle field. When he came out to investigate, the object seemed to move away towards Preston. So odd was the sighting that Mr. Murphy decided to telephone the police and report the incident.

He then returned to the field to check on the cattle, only to find the object return and hover over the area for several more minutes. He became very distressed and, the story goes, called the number for MAPIT (the Manchester Aerial Phenomena Investigation Team) - apparently provided by the police. He left a disturbing message stating that he had witnessed a UFO and was scared.

MAPIT spent weeks investigating the incident, during which time they found themselves being followed by a man in a 4x4 jeep and later discovered that Mr. Murphy had been warned off by officials who claimed to be from the MAFF (Ministry of Agriculture, Fisheries and Food). Mr. Murphy disappeared and has never been traced, making it impossible to corroborate the story. The farm still remains, although the owner has always been reluctant to speak out on the issue.

So famous is the incident that television companies from Britain, America and Japan have all visited MAPIT's HQ to interview the organisation's president, Stephen Mera. He is yet to uncover the full story, although he has also investigated the use of high-tech military equipment - including so-called "black helicopters" which can regularly be seen in the area.

I'm afraid I have no real views on the subject of any Winter Hill sightings only to comment that after a decade of flying a microlight around Winter Hill in all weathers and at all times of day I have never spotted a thing that could not be fully explained. Whilst walking on the hill however, I HAVE spotted a number of people who obviously come from another planet.

You can spot these "aliens" all over the place, causing damage, dropping litter, causing general problems for the more normal inhabitants of the area. There must be an invasion of aliens on the Easter weekends!

Wilderswood and Rockhaven Castle.

On the southern flanks of Winter Hill, lies Wilderswood, a heavily wooded area on the side of the hill south of Georges Lane. To look at the area nowadays one would think that it had always looked like this but this is not the case. The bulk of this area was once bare moorland with few trees (except for the nearby wooded cloughs) and must have been fairly busy with local coal mining activities.

At some past date - unknown to the writer - a house known as Rock Haven was built on the top of the hill which lies behind Brinks Row cottages and in 1840 a Richard Brownlow, a Bolton attorney moved into the property. Over a period of years he rebuilt parts of the house and added various embellishments to it including castle-like parapets and the dwelling eventually became known as Rockhaven Castle, or "Torney Brownlow's Castle.

Richard Brownlow lived at Rock Haven until his death in 1899 but in his latter years he became something of a recluse rarely appearing in public and suffering from a "terrible disease" which involved some form of facial disfigurement. He is reputed to have worn a mask to hide his illness on occasions and local people thought he was suffering from leprosy - but in fact he seems to have had a severe case of eczema.

After Brownlow's death the "castle" passed to the ownership of Lord Leverhulme and eventually in 1940 Blackrod Council put forward plans to turn it into a Youth Hostel but this idea was abandoned and in 1942 it was sold to a local quarry company who eventually demolished it in May 1942. One rumour that I keep hearing, is that the Castle was a prominent landmark for German bombers who were trying to bomb the Horwich Loco Works and this was the reason for its eventual destruction.

The whole site was planted with trees and although I am no great lover of "forestry-type" plantations, a walk through parts of the woodland is a delight today. When walking in the woods one often comes across the remains of parts of the castle along with small quarries where the stones were obtained for the original building. In M D Smith's book "About Horwich" he mentions that after the demolition, some of the stonework was used "to build a bungalow in Lytham whilst the remainder was carried as ballast in grain ships travelling to America". Fascinating!

Coal mining took place in the vicinity and as mentioned in an earlier article there are several tunnel entrances (all blocked or collapsed) to be seen especially in the clough on the north western side of Wilderswood. This valley is well worth a visit especially if one follows the stream uphill. There is an excellent variety of mosses, liverworts and ferns clinging to the banking - and the upper reaches, just south of Georges Lane, are a mecca for whimberry lovers in autumn.

An interesting hour can be spent exploring this area of the clough, starting at the bridge on Dark Lane (also known as Cole-Fire Lane and Rothwells Clough) just inside Wilderswood, which is at the end of the track leading from Ormstons Farm. Mention has already been made earlier to the two collapsed tunnels which can be seen in this vicinity, but as one walks up the main track there are in fact other mining remains, but these have all been totally sealed, some with brickwork and others with cement blocks. A shaft in the area known as Cabin Pit still exists but again, this is sealed. Don't bother searching for it, it is well secured and I can assure readers that there is nothing of interest down it!!

Carry on up the track. On the left hand side is another track. On the small hill in between the two tracks is another old pit shaft, now completely filled in. Nearby are the huge blocks of stone used as engine beds and supports for the machinery involved in winding the coal up the shaft. The counterbalance (a large circular stone with a central hole) for the pit head gear now stands in Ormstons farmyard. The remains of Holden's Bleachworks can be found just to the north west of the pit shaft. Return to the main track in the bottom of the clough.

Go uphill on the main path. Where the path goes to the right through the gateposts, go straight on up the smaller path (i.e. leaving the main track) for a short distance. On the right hand side of the path you will see a large diameter metal pipe sticking out of the ground. This was an air vent to the mines below. Although clearly marked on mining maps, the base of this pipe has never been found (it is a bit of a maze underground so it is no surprise that the bottom of the pipe has not been found – yet!). Carry on up the path.

There is a prominent large holly tree on the left hand side of the track. Behind the tree lies the remains of Higher Meadows Farm, the foundations of which are still visible in the undergrowth. Careful searching will reveal half of what appears to be the bottom section of an old grinding wheel.

Opposite the holly tree but down in the bottom of the clough, is a magnificent clump of wild iris growing in the waterlogged ground, a beautiful sight when in full flower. "Somewhere" in the clough is the entrance to an old mine marked as "old level" on old maps. Despite frequent and extensive searches, this tunnel entrance has never been found despite its map location.

Carry on up the path until you reach another main track which leads up to Georges Lane. On the left hand side of this track, beneath

Georges Lane are two "valleys" which look very artificial and are repeated many times on this hillside if one headed towards the Pike. These are thought to be old surface workings for either coal or clay although no proof of this has yet been found. This hillside is a magnet for whimberry pickers every autumn!

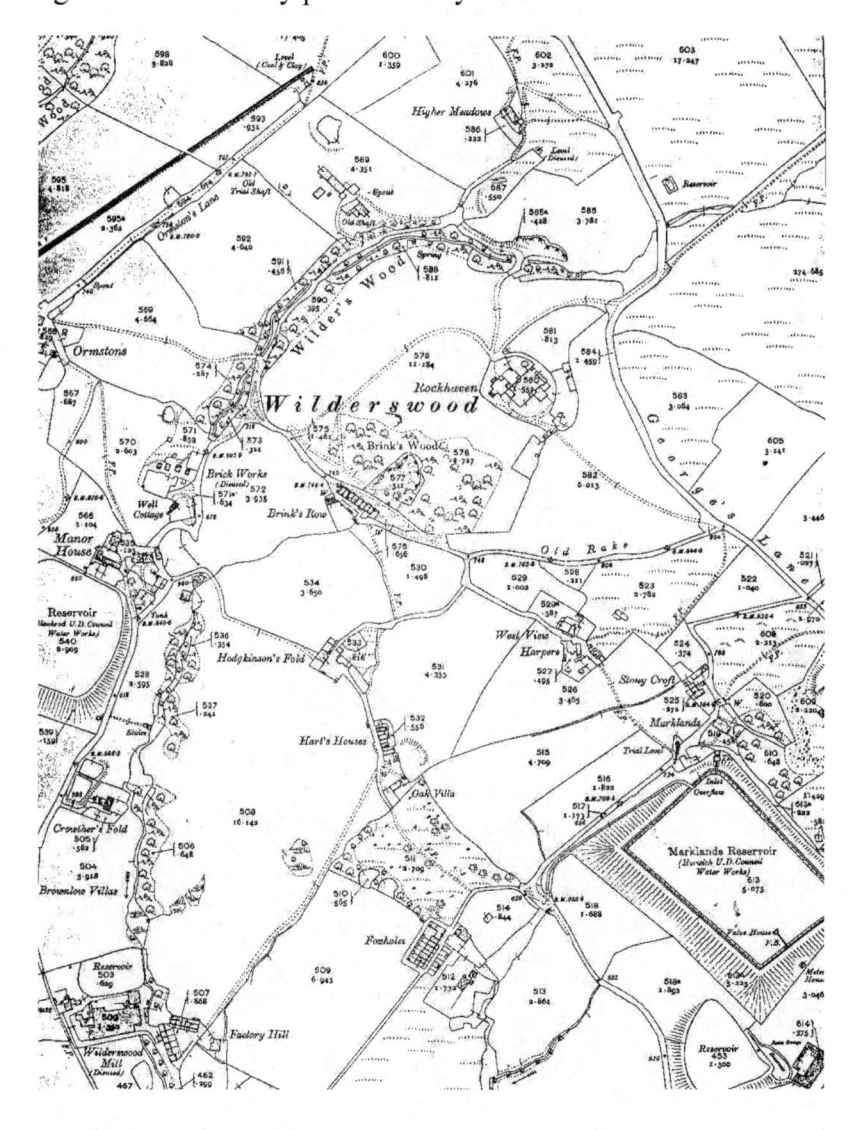

1907 map of the Wilderswood area.

The old or "disused" level mentioned in the last article can be seen just to the right of Higher Meadows Farm – clearly marked on the map but now vanished! The dark diagonal line at the upper left hand corner is the tramway to the Wilderswood Mine Drift entrance.

The Royal Wedding Beacon. Winter Hill. July 21st 1981.

Royal Wedding beacons

To Hecla, St Kilda

To Fair Isle, Bressay, Saxa Void

ITES of 102 beacons to be set alight in a chain across Britain n the Royal Wedding eve after Prince Charles lights the first t 10pm during a firework display in Hyde Park attended by he Queen and Prince Philip. Fires will be lit in sequence at ocations spanning 850 miles from Jersey to the Shetlands.

HE SUNDAY TELEGRAPH. SUNDAY, JUNE 21 1981

Rivington Pike and Winter Hill have been used as beacon sites for hundreds of years. Perhaps the most memorable beacon at these sites was in 1981 at the time of the wedding of Charles and Diana. A chain of beacons was planned around the country

On the night of the beacon, the two-mile uphill track from Horwich to the Trig point on Winter Hill (where the bonfire was located) was jammed with revellers who slogged to the top of the hill for the official lighting time of 10.19pm. The beacon was "officially" lit by 10 year old spina bifada sufferer Janet Lomax of Hillfield Drive, Bolton. She was given VIP treatment and driven through the crowds of walkers to the site along with the mayors and mayoresses from surrounding towns. Many people arrived late – or even missed the lighting of the fire as it had been wrongly announced in the Press, that it was at Rivington Pike! This caused total chaos on the Rivington/Belmont road which was blocked till the early hours by trapped vehicles.

The beacon was built by the Royal Institute of Chartered Surveyors and was around 30 feet in height.

The beacon was no "jerry-built" job as can be seen by the photo of the frame.

It was estimated that over 5,000 people made it to the top of the hill in time to see its lighting only a few hundred yards from the TV mast. The sight of the flames ended a nail-biting 24 hours for the beacon builder Peter Veevers and his helpers who camped out on the moor to ensure there was no premature lighting. The team had brought wood up the hill twice every week over a two-month period to prepare for the bonfire.

It was an enjoyable and memorable occasion for all those who were there.

Flying at Winter Hill

A great deal of flying takes place on, around and over Winter Hill!

There are the commercial flights that pass high over Winter Hill. The LOWEST height they are allowed to fly over the Hill is 3,500 feet. Smaller general aviation aircraft (such as those from Barton Aerodrome) have to keep BELOW this height and can often be seen in the area along with microlights and the occasional powered paraglider. In theory, these aircraft must remain above 800 feet from the ground.

Flying from the hill itself are hang gliders and paragliders, usually on days when the wind is in a northerly direction and not too windy and they fly on the northern side of the hill, overlooking the Rivington/Belmont road. On a busy weekend in summer I have seen up to 40 people flying at the site and if the thermals are good an awful lot of them seem to fly in close proximity to each other vying for the best updraughts! Most of the pilots belong to local hang or paragliding clubs with details easily found on the Internet via a search engine.

The hill is also the "home" of the Rivington Soaring Association, a group of model glider enthusiasts who use both the Southern slopes of Rivington Pike and the Northern Slopes of Winter Hill. They have a web site at: http://www.sar.bolton.ac.uk/ian/rsa.htm

Fireclay on (and under) Winter Hill.

In earlier volumes, mention has been made of fireclay (sometimes known as Seat-earth) being found below (and sometimes in a tiny layer above) coal seams. This material is especially relevant as in earlier days, it played a considerable role in the industries and ventures that sprung up on and around Winter Hill.

Fireclay is a grey muddy clay. It usually lies below most coal seams and on Winter Hill many of the mining ventures were specifically for fireclay - with coal being almost a by-product. Coal was formed by compression of decaying vegetation existing in swamp-like areas. The fireclay represents the sediment or soil in which the swamp vegetation grew.

The clay is rich in alumina content and is an excellent material for the manufacture of firebricks used in kilns and smelting. The clay was also used in the making of salt-glazed pipes and sanitary-ware until the late 1950's when it was superseded by more modern materials. There were a number of sanitary product manufacturers in Horwich earlier in the 19th & 20th centuries all using the clay mined from underneath Winter Hill.

You can still find the remains of some of the brickworks on the Hill, with perhaps the one at Hole Bottom being the most easily accessible. Firebricks still remain there, all made from the local clay. An excellent example of locally made firebricks can found right at the summit of Winter Hill where a number are stacked next to - and on top of - the boundary wall adjacent to the most southerly radio mast. A photo of the wall can be seen on the next page.

In several places on the Hill, the fireclay can be seen on the surface. The best example I have recently seen, is in a small "shakehole" (formed by the collapse of an underground adit tunnel) about 300 yards to the rear of Sportsmans cottage and around 50 yards from the boundary wall on the top bank of the nearby stream. The grey clay can be found on the sides of the hole and can be taken home, moulded and baked. The collapsed adit tunnel used to exit on the on the banks of the nearby stream but is now totally filled in and covered in vegetation. It is clearly marked on mine abandonment plans.

There is also another clay outcrop near to the TV mast on top of Winter Hill (see the article about the "other Brickworks" elsewhere in this book).

All of the coal seams on Winter Hill are underlain with a seam of fireclay.

Firebricks near to the most southerly radio mast on top of Winter Hill.

The layer of grey fireclay can be clearly seen below the coal seam. This picture was taken under the summit of Winter Hill fairly close to

the moorland road leading to the TV mast. This tunnel is now not accessible and this may be the last picture you ever see of it.

The Cranberries …. Where are they?

Since writing the earlier volumes, a number people have contacted me enquiring about the exact locations of various types of plants growing on the Hill. Where specific plants are numerous, I have given exact locations, where they are rare, I have been deliberately vague! By far the most asked question is "Exactly where are the cranberries on Winter Hill"? I'm still not prepared to disclose exactly where they are - but the photo below of the flower of the cranberry may help. Bear in mind that the flower and stem are only just over an inch high. Once you've seen a cranberry flower in real life you'll recognise it instantly anywhere.

The flower of the cranberry. The petals curl backwards towards stem. The leaves are those tiny insignificant things on the bottom left of the photo.

The flowers appear between late May and early July ….. and if you often walk on the very top of Winter Hill I'm willing to bet that at sometime or another you'll have passed within 10 foot of them!

When you've found the cranberries, then you can start looking for the Cloud Berries!

If you can't find the cranberries OR the Cloud Berries, then there are simply acres of whimberries for you to pick! Bon Appetit.

More about the Lichens of Winter Hill.

Probably one of the most ignored organisms on Winter Hill are the lichens in all its different guises. The grasses, mosses, shrubs and trees are all too obvious to most observers, but somehow the lichens get overlooked or ignored by most folk interested in the plant life of the area. You tend to only take note of them, once they've been pointed out.

Lichens can exist in the most unlikely places even in spots where no other plant life grows - such as directly on the surface of rocks or bricks. They are complex plants rather than being simple as most people imagine, and are something of a mini ecosystem consisting of at least two life-forms, a fungus and a photosynthetic partner which is usually an algae (but can be others things as well). Lichens can exist in extreme environments and often grow under conditions that other plant life cannot tolerate.

"Weathering" on walls and rocks usually turns out to be lichen growth on closer inspection. Carrying a tiny hand lens when you go walking on Winter Hill can prove more interesting than you imagine - although you sometimes feel a real fool kneeling down to use it near other people.

There are many different types of lichen, a number of which can be seen right on the very top of Winter Hill, the most obvious ones being the "crustose" or "parmelia" ones growing on the walls and stones. These come in many colours, usually grey, slightly green, brown or even orange, perhaps even black dotted - and different species seem to inhabit different areas on different parts of the hill. Most of the ancient walls on the Hill seem to have coloured blotches - usually put down to "weathering" - are in fact lichens upon closer inspection.

Forms of the "reindeer moss" types of lichens, "pixie cup" lichens are all to be found on top of the Hill. Perhaps the most colourful variety to search for is the "British soldier", a bright red tipped member of the "cladonia" family which is easily spotted from June onwards on Winter Hill. All of these types of lichens can be found within 100 yards of the Hole Bottom brickworks. In this vicinity I have also spotted a lichen I have never ever seen anywhere else in the area, it grows on one of the bricks which once formed the inside of one of the brick kilns, a sort of melted looking stone.

If anyone can identify this lichen for me I'd love to hear from you!

Two photo's of "British Soldier" types of lichen - fairly common in the Hole Bottom area. The name originated with the red caps worn by British soldiers in earlier centuries. The plants red caps are actually the sexual fruiting structure of the lichen, the apothecia. British soldiers are members of the "Cladonia" family of lichens.

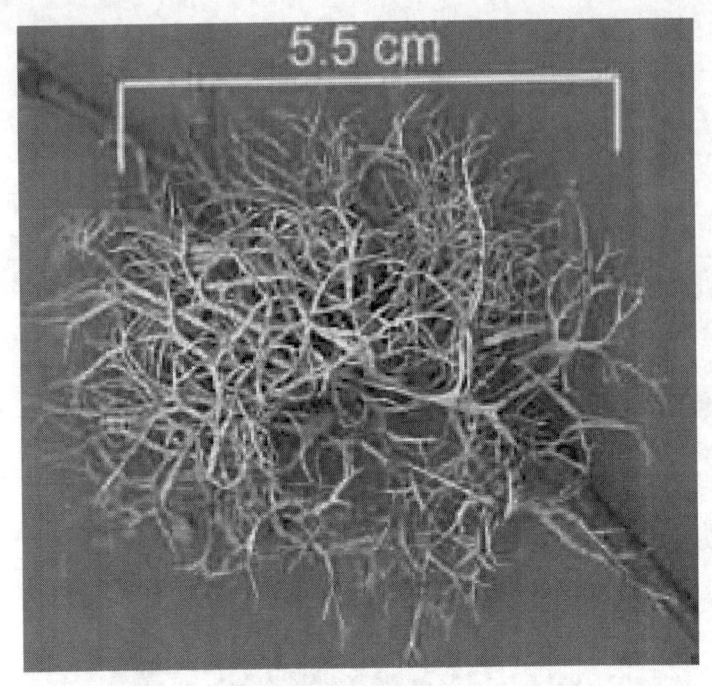

A lichen similar to those found on Winter Hill - although the maximum size I have ever found right at the top is about 1 inch in size. The usual variety found on Winter Hill is "Cladonia Arbuscula".

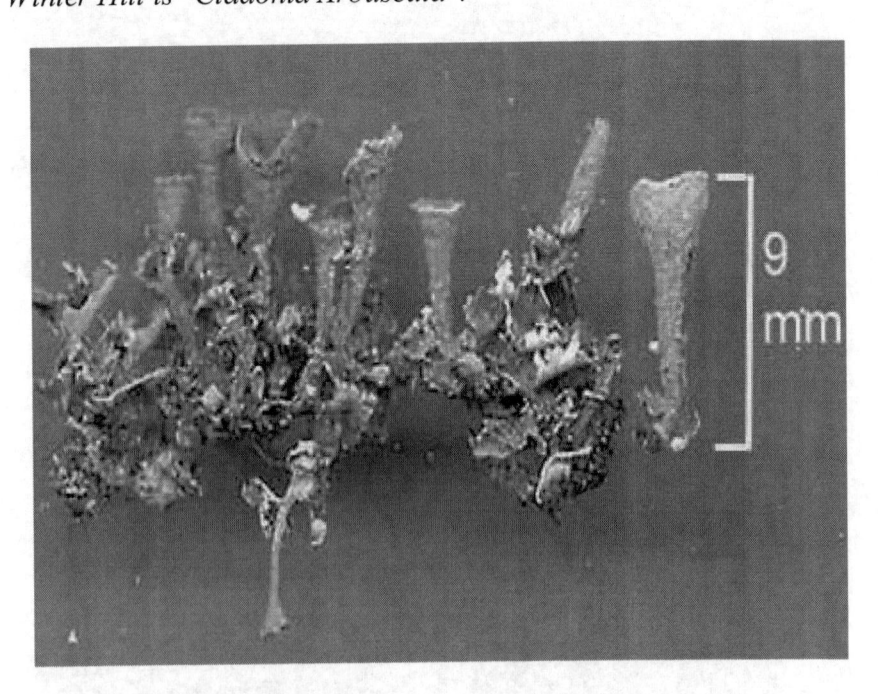

One of the Pixie Cup varieties, extremely common amongst the heather in many places on Winter Hill. Often grows in close proximity to the British soldiers.

One of the commonest lichens growing on the lower flanks of Winter Hill, Hypogymnia Physodes, usually on tree bark.

The sheep of Winter Hill.

When most people think of a sheep, they think of ... well .... a sheep! They all look the same don't they? Actually no they don't - and there are hundreds of different types of sheep in the fields, on the hills and mountains of the British Isles. Different varieties of sheep are grown for different purposes (some for meat, some for wool, others for breeding) and some types fare better in different environments.

Sheep are both a blessing and a curse on Winter Hill. They are a blessing because they look nice, they sound nice, they eat what's left of my butties to save me taking them home and most importantly, they provide a livelihood for local farmers. They are a curse because they seem to eat everything and the Hill looks as it does now, mainly because of the sheep. Unless an area is fenced off, no trees or shrubs grow, they are quickly devoured. Where sheep are present, the vegetation is usually very short and certain plant species are unable to survive the continuous close grazing. The presence of sheep maintains the generally deforested top of Winter Hill.

There are three main varieties of sheep grazing on Winter Hill.

"Derbyshire Gritstone", a mountain and hill variety which is found mainly in Derbyshire and the Pennine Districts of Lancashire & Yorkshire with a few also found in Wales. They are distinguished by their faces and legs being white with black markings and there is no wool growing on these parts either. They are hornless. Their wool is one of the finest of all grown by the blackfaced type of sheep and it is extensively used in the high quality hosiery business.

Also seen on the Hill is the Swaledale, dark upper face with grey muzzle and a tuft of wool on the forehead. Both sexes are horned. It is found in the fells, moorlands and high ground of the six counties of Northern England and it lives easily in exposed places.

Many Swaledale ewes are used for breeding the very popular Mules, and the finer quality wool from this breed of sheep (the Swaledales that is!) is used for the manufacture of tweeds, rug wool and some of the thicker hand-knitting wools. Much of the wool is of coarse quality but this is ideal for the making of carpets.

The final variety found on the Hill is the Cheviot.

The Cheviot is distinguishable by its erect ears, white face and legs with a ruff of wool behind the ears. There is no wool on the face or legs below the knee or hock. The males are occasionally horned. The wool quality varies from fairly course to quite fine and is used for manufacture into clothing - ranging from rugged sportswear to lighter town suitings. Cheviot wool is also used for making blankets, rugs and hosiery yarns.

You need never again wonder what type the sheep are on Winter Hill! However, just to confuse you, the breeds listed are only those you will find on the Hill itself - in the fields on the lower flanks of the Hill you will also find Mules, Dalesbred and Lonks plus a few other crossbreed varieties.

The sheep on the upper parts of the hill are free to roam and are brought back down the hill several times a year for mating (known as "tupping") usually around October/early November, lambing around April and for clipping in June/July. They may also be brought off the hill for dipping and worming although some farms dip the flock at clipping time, whilst others delay the dipping for a month or so until a little fleece has re-grown.

Don't forget .... whilst on the hills, KEEP YOUR DOG under control especially at and prior to lambing time. Your dog's hour of freedom could mean the death or abortion of a lamb and a financial loss to the farmer. Be considerate!

Dalesbred - distinguishable by its black face with distinct white mark at either side of its nostrils. The legs are also black and white and they have a rounded low set pair of horns. The fleece is tough and springy and is ideal for making carpet yarns. Dalesbred can survive in the bleakest conditions and on the roughest pastures.

More ancient remains from Winter Hill.

In an earlier volume I mentioned that someone had written to me saying that some years ago they had found a flint spear or axe in the vicinity of the Winter Hill Burial Mound. Thanks for the info John McDonald. Several weeks after receiving the information - and after the last volume had been finished a computer scan of the object turned up in my mailbox. Wow ..... what a magnificent find.

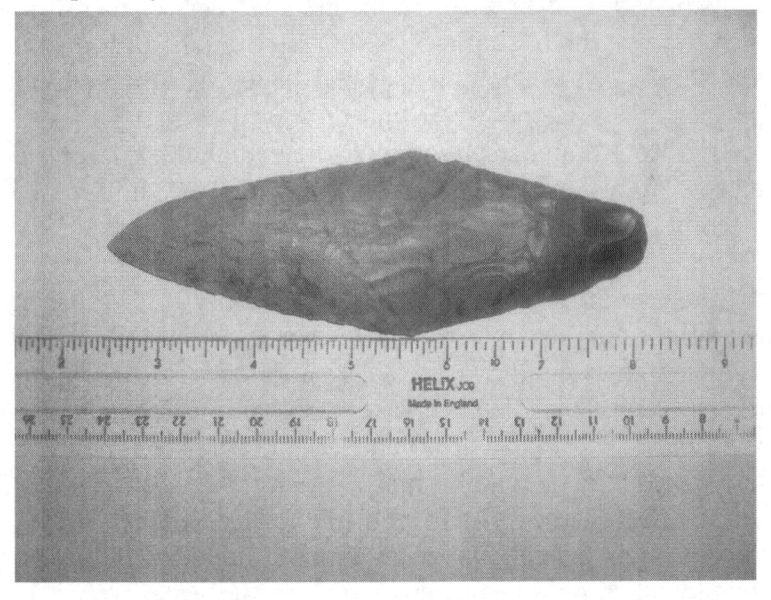

This is a five and a half inch long axe head, in what looks like excellent condition. Why is it that everyone else seems to find flint chippings, flint arrowheads, flint axes etc on Winter Hill ... except me! Thanks for the excellent photograph John, you lucky devil!

There are by the way, several well known sites (at least they are well known within archaeological circles) on Winter Hill where flint chippings have been found in some quantities. These would be areas where someone once sat whilst working on a block of flint producing arrowheads, spears, scrapers etc. These sites are marked on copies of a few privately produced maps. I have still found nothing! Any additional photo's of other peoples "finds" would be appreciated.

Gritstone - what is it - and how was it formed.

When you look at rocks on the summit of Winter Hill, they all look the same, a dark coloured, rough textured, gritty or sandy rock. The term "grit" is a useful - if non-scientific" - term for a course sandstone. There are of course other types of rock around, but by far the most predominant one is the substance some people call "millstone grit". The term "millstone grit" does in fact (in geology) refer to a whole "series" of massive and different layers of sandstone's, grits, conglomerates and shales. The type of rock - or the "species" of gritstone - you find on top of Winter Hill is known as "Rough Rock", a coarsely grained stone containing large amounts of feldspar and is sparsely pebbly. Lower down the hill you will find a different type of Gritstone…. the "Haslingden Flags".

The dark colouring of the rock is due mainly to "weathering" - and the pollution in this industrial area - break a piece open and inside it's a much lighter colour. This is a grittier type of the rock than that usually termed "sandstone". Take a look at it under a small hand lens. Are most of the grains are rounded? - if they are, this indicates that they were almost certainly transported by water (or in some cases by wind) which quickly removed the rough edges. If the sample contains only jagged or rough grains, then this indicates that the granules have only been transported by the water over a very short distance without being subjected to "rounding".

The rocks of the area were formed during the Carboniferous period (especially during the Namurian phase of that era), that is somewhere around 290 to 363 million years ago. How do we know this age? We know it by the study of a mixture of geological evidence, the study of the stratigraphic structures, the fossil remains, the study of the radioactive decay rates of rocks and finally by the modern technique of paleomagnetic studies.

Gritstones consists of rock particles transported by water. Different areas of Winter Hill show massive differences in the sizes of the grains transported and deposited, the size usually indicating the relative strength of the current - the larger particles usually being deposited in strong current flows, with the finer particles settling as the current strength decreased. Different sandstone's or Grits at different places on the Hill show a wide variety of colours and grain sizes. The "Rough Rock" on the top of Winter Hill almost certainly originated as sands or mineral grains - probably brought from as far away as Scandinavia and Greenland - were deposited near the mouth of a massive delta.

Park your car in the **upper** car park at Lower House car park (that's the one below the Pigeon Tower at the end of the road leading from Rivington Road). Take the footpath going north from the car park and on the right hand side of the path, drop into the small dry valley. After a few minutes walking, you'll spot some small gritstone or sandstone/mudstone outcrops on your right hand side. Take a look at the rocks. The first thing you'll notice is that the rocks appear to be layered horizontal beds of sediment. This indicates repeated "floods" of varying strengths over a period of time, maybe years - or even centuries, maybe millennia. Different floods deposited different sizes of granules and these can all be seen in the revealed strata. In this particular example, the flows seem to have been of different strengths at different times. Some strata contain large rounded rocks amongst the small grains, other layers are totally graded fine granules. Some layers are very thin, some are much thicker. Perhaps each "layer" represents a major "flood" each year … your guess is as good as mine as to what the layers actually represent.

The layers of sandstone (or "grits") in this locality show conspicuous signs of "current bedding", indicating that they were deposition in deltaic environments i.e. at a place where a large river delta was depositing the solids brought down by its waters.

How did the granules turn into "rocks"? The various layers of silt and granules were endlessly covered by yet more layers. As they became thicker and thicker, the pressure on them increased, and they became compressed. There were still spaces between the grains or granules. These spaces were however often filled with moisture or water and this, combined with the increased pressure and its associated heat, caused chemical changes in some of the substances within the sediment. The quartz grains remained the same, but if there was any $CaCO_3$, $Fe(OH)_3$ or SiO_2 present, then the warmth and the pressure would precipitate these chemicals and "glue" the deposits together. That is how the "rock" was formed - through compression, water, heat and chemical action. The major "cement" is silica (a form of quartz), others "cements" include calcite (only recognisable with a chemical test) and iron compounds (shown by their rusty red colour). The strength of the "cement" governs how easily grains may be broken away from the rock. Most Winter Hill cements are strong!

Occasionally (VERY occasionally!) plants or trees were swept down these torrents, and these remains formed fossils, but these are rare in most forms of sandstone (or gritstone) in this area. After years of searching I have only found only one such sandstone fossil, this being part of a tree trunk - found at Black Hill, north of Anglezarke. It is course possible that "my" fossil came from Winter Hill and was carried to Anglezarke by later glacial action - although as the local glaciers tended to go from North to South this possibility fairly remote!

Don't bother looking for dinosaur fossils …. Dinosaurs would appear on earth 100 million years later than "our" rocks were formed - and the rocks containing dinosaur fossils were (if they ever existed) in this area, eroded away millions of years ago by either wind, water or ice!

Oh one other thing. Right now, the UK lies at about 53 degrees north of the equator. When our carboniferous and millstone grit series of rocks was being formed, our country lay ON the equator, Winter "Hill" would have been really hot! Over the period since then, plate techtonic movements have moved our Hill (and most of Europe) about 5cms a year northwards, until today - when it reached it's present location.

How time flies!

A Victorian engraving of Rivington Pike. *The date is unknown, but it appeared in a book called "England in the Nineteenth Century" page 280. Note the church with the small steeple at the left hand of the Pike*

Another Winter Hill Brickworks.

In an earlier volume, a description was given about the Winter Hill Brickwork's at Hole Bottom. This is not the only brickwork to have been located on the Hill and in past centuries there were several, many working at the same time. The Hole Bottom brickwork is in an easily accessible place - but some of the other ones are in fairly remote locations.

One of the remote ones is much higher up the hill. To find what remains of it, go up the moorland road from Montcliff towards the TV mast. A few hundred yards before reaching the TV station you will spot a wire fenced off area on the left hand side of the road (this used to be the site of a small wooden hut where the TV station employees used to move to in inclement weather many years ago). Take the track behind the fenced off area, cross over the battered wooden bridge across the ditch and head straight ahead to the brow of the hill. When you get there, look down and you will spot the mounds of the brickwork below. It is easily recognised as the vegetation of the site is different from the surrounding moor.

The view of the brickwork's from half way down the hill. There is no sign of any path or track leading to the site.

Taking a look around the site gives a few clues to exactly what may have been there years ago. There are two mounds on the site, both covered in vegetation. Whether these are both the remains of brick kilns or whether the site had only one kiln plus one building cannot be determined without considerable digging. The smaller mound on the left of the picture was almost certainly a kiln for traces of fused brick (those forming the inside of the kiln) can be spotted nearby. There are also two spits of raised earth heading downhill from this mound which I had long suspected as being where the kiln ash and cinders were tipped. On my latest visit to the site a large rabbit/fox or other large animal had very kindly dug a hole into the side of these raised areas exposing solid ash, clinker and cinders. My theory was proved right without having to do any digging around.

The site appears to have manufactured common bricks and perhaps stoneware items as well. There are several piles of bricks lying around and a number of either complete or broken sinks can also be seen.

It seems from looking at the site, that the clay was obtained from the immediate area surrounding the kilns and in several places the rather poor clay is exposed. I can find no traces of any underground entrances although from the surface collapses I suspect that some of the clay may have been taken from just beneath the surface. I have not checked the geology maps for this exact site but there were surface coal outcrops in this vicinity so the brickwork would have its own clay and coal almost on its doorstep this probably being the reason for its isolated position.

The biggest mound on the site, whilst it "may" have been a kiln shows little real evidence of it so far - despite someone having had a dig into it at some time (it wasn't me). Without striping some of the soil and vegetation off it is impossible to guess any more.

If you have "Google Earth" in your computer, look at Winter Hill at its largest magnification and you'll clearly see this brickworks.

The Bog!

One area of Winter Hill seems to get few visitors whatever the time of year even during the warm days of summer. This is not perhaps surprising for this area appears to have nothing whatsoever to offer anyone and even a map shows nothing more than the words "Winter Hill Springs". Thousands of people walk the footpath between Rivington Pike and the TV mast, and lesser numbers travel between both these places via the Winter Hill Trig point and Noon Hill. Virtually everyone ignores the "empty area" between the two routes.

If you're just intent on getting from point A to point B then there is of course no reason to visit the "empty-quarter" but I have to admit to having a fascination for the place. I love the solitude, the views, the weather, the plants, mosses and lichens that grow there ..... and of course ..... the Bog!

Bogs on Winter Hill come in all shapes and sizes. There is the real muddy bog, the one where one second you're walking on firm ground then within a split second one foot sinks to the thigh in glutinous mud which often has a powerfully bad odour as well. **This** is a normal bog - a trap for the unwary!

Then we have the other type of bog, the "sitting water" bog. This is a place which is an obvious bog, a place where you know that you're going to get your feet wet unless you carefully try to step from one bit of dry or raised grass to the next. The worst that will happen in this type of place is that you just could get wet up to mid calf. This type of bog is also a normal bog!

There is however a different type of bog in many areas surrounding the Winter Hill Springs in the "empty-quarter". This type of bog I class as the "quivering bog" and is an experience not to be missed! I kid you not! These are areas which tend to be fairly flat, well populated by cotton grass in summer, the ground surface appears to be damp or wet and there are considerable clumps of sphagnum moss all over the place. Now this is still a "bog" but you CAN walk on it without getting your feet wet even though it feels decidedly dodgy and a bit "iffy". There is one acid test to see if you've found a "quivering bog". Stand still, keep both feet on the ground but move your BODY up and down fairly rapidly. The surface of the ground around you will start moving up and down in time with your body movements. If you've chosen a particularly good area to do your strange body movements, the ground ripples will appear all round you to a distance of perhaps up to 10 feet away. It's quite a sight, and boy, does it feel odd! The exact location of this bog is at SD 65063 14753.

The explanation as to why this "quivering" or "rippling" happens just may put you off trying in the first place, but what the heck, live dangerously and try it! The quivering bog is liquid glutinous mud but this is topped by a thin layer of fairly firm peat and plant life. The surface is safe enough to walk on and jump up and down on, but your body movements are enough to start movements in the liquid mud beneath, and these movements can affect a considerable area of surface peat around the spot where you are gyrating! This then is the "quivering bog"!

I do all MY gyrating at the edges of this type of bog. I take no responsibility whatsoever if any **20** stone person decides to test the quivering in the MIDDLE of such a bog, just so see if he/she can extend the quivering area to a **20** foot radius! Such a person has to be mentally deficit.

Sphagnum Moss

Whilst you're in the area take a look at the sphagnum mosses. You can't confuse sphagnum with any other type of moss. They are "mat" plants the topmost, live part, consisting of rosettes of densely packed branches facing upwards. The "mat" builds on itself, accumulating an underneath branch depth of several inches or feet, browning and dying close to the surface, decaying lower down. The only "live" part of the plant is the green (they can be other colours too) bit at the top, the dead part of the "stems" are merely used to "wick" up the water to the living part of the plant.

Sphagnum moss can store or hold large amounts of water - if you grab a small handful and squeeze it tightly, large amounts of water will run from it - even in the dry seasons sometimes. Sphagnum moss acts as a sponge and can hold 10 times its own weight in water both internally and in the spaces between the dense foliage. There are 30 different species of sphagnum moss in the British Isles and if you keep your eyes open in the "empty quarter" you should be able to spot at least 6 different types purely from their visual appearance alone, size, colour, composition of rosette etc.

Sphagnum Cristatum

A single sphagnum moss plant is very small but it grows packed together with other sphagnum plants and they provide support for each others tiny stems. This produces a soft spongy carpet which can, on occasions, look like a colourful patchwork, as each kind of sphagnum moss has its own shade of colour ranging from light green, through orange, pink, white and red.

The Coal Mines of Rivington Pike!

In the first part of this Scrapbook, mention was made of two coal mine shafts to the north of Rivington Pike plus a nearby level - all now long since filled in and virtually unseen today.

There are however, other coal mining remains nearer to the Pike - and you can still see the remains!

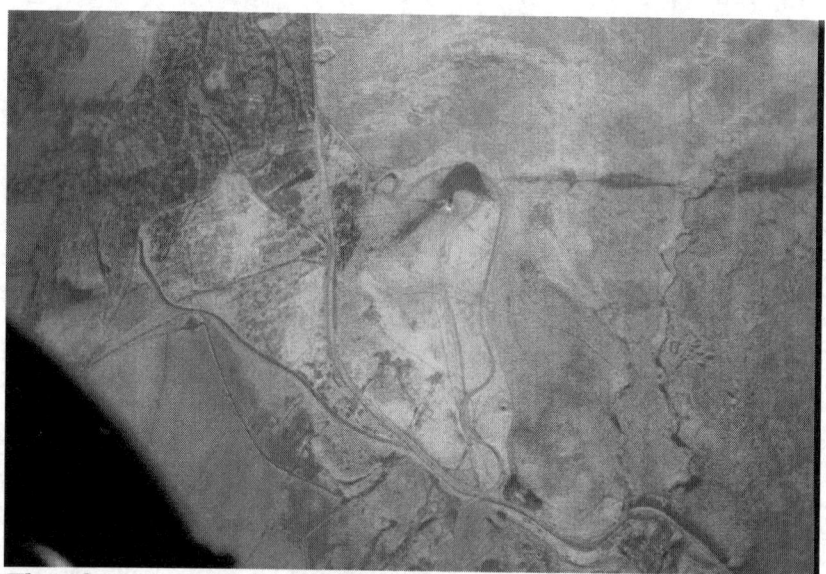

The photo is a rather poor quality winter aerial view of the area surrounding Rivington Pike, the Pike being upper centre. On the right of the picture can be seen mining remains on the right hand bank of the stream. The "crater" on the right hand side of the road going up to the Pike at the base of Brown Hill is an old mine shaft. Just to the right of extreme bottom centre of the photo are what looks like 3 more pits - but these are in fact the remains of an old farmhouse!.

Surrounding the Pike is a coal outcrop, an area where the coal seam emerged at the surface. In the early 1800's (or even earlier) this coal would have been worked using "bell pits" and it is this type of pit which is clearly evident on the banks of the stream on the right hand side of the photo. The dark oblong shape near the pits is the remains of a stone structure, probably a sheep fold. A further photograph taken at ground level (on the next page) clearly shows the sheepfold (or whatever it was) with the heavily mined ground at the rear of it.

I have no details whatsoever about the pit shaft visible near to the road up to the Pike, nor the ones next to George's Lane at the bottom of the photo.

The "sheepfold" with the coal workings at the rear.

Just when you thought you'd heard everything there was to know about Winter Hill ……….. well, now I've found THIS on the UFO Information web page at:
http://www.ufoinfo.com/news/humanoid1950.shtml

Location. Winter Hill, near Bolton, England
Date: 1950
Time: night
The witness, R Chapman sees a dark flat iron shaped object hovering close to the ground. Suddenly out of nowhere a "majestic" being

appears. He is tall, well built, with black hair and beard, dark eyes and very pale skin. There is telepathic contact between Chapman and the humanoid for several minutes. The humanoid then turns around and glides back to the UFO apparently decreasing in size as he did. After he enters the craft the UFO leaves leaving a vapour trail behind. The witness apparently encounters the same being again at the same location. (No details on that).
HC addendum
Source: Gemini Vol. 1 # 2
Type: B

Not much one can add!!!!!!

This photo is said to be taken on Winter Hill – but I suspect it is the Chipmunk which crashed on Smithills Moor.

Winter on Winter Hill!

More Winter Hill mining remains! This view shows the "quarries" at the side of the Rivington to Belmont road (which can be seen at the extreme bottom left of the picture). Pit shafts everywhere! Notice the "tilled" field on the right hand side ... what on earth could have been grown there ....And when? This site housed a gun emplacement during WW2 used for target practice - firing straight across the road! Hundreds of mortars were recovered from the fields across the road about 20 years ago! Tread carefully!

Matchmoor Riding Centre.

Hidden away on the flanks of Winter Hill is a real "treasure" of the area, the riding school on Matchmoor Lane (Matchmoor Lane is the first road on the right hand side of Georges Lane after leaving the main Horwich Road. It's about 100 yards up the lane hidden away on the left hand side of the road. It's no use looking for the stables for they are partly sunken below the road level and you could easily drive past the place.

After almost two years of watching my grandchildren learn to ride there, I can assure you that this is a real friendly place and everyone seems to be welcome there both adults and children, total beginners and experienced riders. It's been in existence for over 20 years and they have over 30 horses. You can take horse riding lessons there or you can join a "hack" going out in a group into the countryside surrounding the riding centre. On a clear day the views are superb.

They seem to run rides and courses in just about everything, from hacks, class lessons, private lessons, stable management lessons, children's holiday courses, BHS Riding and Road Safety courses and Stage 1, 2 & 3 career courses. They even cater for children's birthday parties.

The horses and ponies used range from Shetlands through to throughbreds with many sure-footed Mountain and Moorland ponies.

The Riding Centre is open all day, every day and you can book a lesson on **01204 693323**. The emphasis is on enjoyment - whether you just want to learn to ride or to improve your existing skills.

The one thing that has always struck me about this place is the friendliness of all who work there - and I take my hat off to the instructor who teaches my grandchildren, she remains cheerful, offers constant encouragement and praise whatever is happening and whatever the weather.

The prices are reasonable (prices correct as at March 2005):
Half hour hack	£5
Hour hack	£7.50
Half hour group lesson	£7.00
Day hack	£30.00

Yet another ancient find on the Hill!

Following publication of Volume 2 of the Winter Hill Scrapbook I received an email from David Aspinall, who is the person who discovered and wrote about the stone rows on Winter Hill - which are described in this volume of the Scrapbook.

David kindly sent me the pictures shown below. These illustrate a stone scraper found in the vicinity of "his" stone rows. The stone was found by someone else ... who unfortunately does not live in the Bolton area .... So this picture is probably the only record of the item which will be seen by Boltonians. If YOU have found anything ... send me a picture!

A wonderful old painting of Rivington Pike and Two Lads

(Many thanks to Wigan Leisure and Culture Trust, Dept of Heritage Archives for permission to show this copyrighted picture)

Sportsman's Cottage .... Date unknown

The "Geo-Caches" of Winter Hill.

What is a Geocache? ...... "The basic idea is to have individuals and organisations set up caches all over the world and share the locations of these caches on the internet. GPS users can then use the location co-ordinates to find the caches. Once found, a cache may provide the visitor with a wide variety of rewards. All the visitor is asked to do is if they get something they should try to leave something for the cache". That's the official description as laid out on the official geo-caching web site at: http://www.geocaching.com/

In practice geo-caching involves the finding of hidden containers of various types and sizes by using a hand held GPS (Global Positioning System) unit. These caches are hidden literally all over the world and there are thousands of them all over the UK. Some of them are merely 35mm film canisters with a really TINY visitors book inside .... These are usually known as "mini cache's". Other caches are substantial plastic containers or old ammunition cases which contain all sorts of gifts and other assorted junk! If you TAKE an item from the cache you MUST replace it with something.

Almost ALL cache's have a visitors book to sign and when you've found a cache it is good manners to log on to the www.geocaching.com web site to leave a message there also. In this way the person who hid the cache in the first place can get instant feedback on his computer as to who has visited it.

There are MANY caches both on and around Winter Hill but you'll have to go to the "Hide and Seek a cache" page on the Geo-caching web site and have a root around to see what is available. As this is being written, I can see caches listed on the top of Winter Hill, Rivington Pike and many more nearby. New one's pop up all the time so any list given here would soon be out of date.

Take a look for them! It's great fun, a real excuse to get out in the fresh air and see new places and kids just love it.

A documentary film called "Scotsman's Stump" has been made about the murder of George Henderson on Winter Hill. Further details can be found at: http://reelvisionfilms.co.uk/shop.html

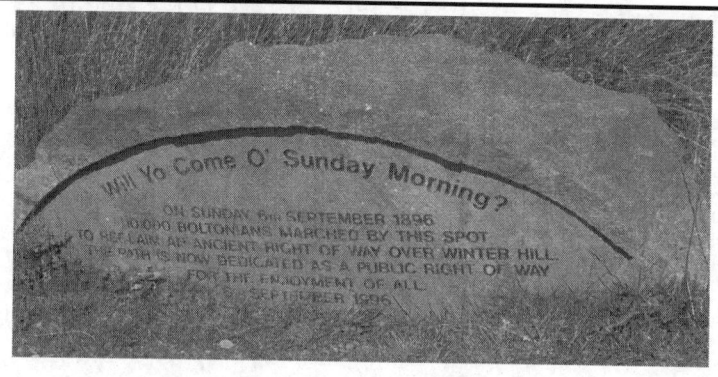

The Memorial Stone erected in 1996 to commemorate the centenary of the Winter Hill Mass Trespass of 1896. (photo courtesy of Eric Hewis)

One of the Winter Hill tunnel entrances. Do NOT attempt to enter this lethal mine (photo courtesy of David Swain).

Shown below is a QSL card (a confirmation that someone has either heard or seen transmissions sent by either a radio amateur or an experimental station) concerning experimental TV transmissions from Winter Hill. The experiments were conducted in 1956 and the card is from "Experimental TV station G9AED located on Winter Hill map ref 34/660149". The card quotes "Channel 9" as being used with vision on 194.75 Mc/s and audio on 191.25 Mc/s.

Past Vegetation on and around Winter Hill.

An earlier article tells the geological history of Winter Hill and many mentions are made throughout the book of how the plant life of the area has changed over time. However, no real mention has been made of the major vegetative changes that have taken place on and around Winter Hill over the last 10,000 years or so. This information can be obtained by the study and dating of pollen grains found within peat and in peat bogs.

The following extract from an article entitled "Past Vegetation, Future Global Warming?" by Robert Yates, Chairman of the West Pennine Moors Conservation Committee from 1983 to 2000.

"In Chorley, we are fortunate to have on our doorstep at Red Moss, Horwich, *(which is adjacent to the Middlebrook/Reebok Shopping Centre)* one of the best studied sites of peat deposition in the whole of the British Isles. Pollen analysis from Red Moss gives us a picture of the vegitational history of the area and therefore an understanding of past climatic changes. Perhaps they can give us a clue to future developments.

Since the end of the Pliocene, some 2 million years ago, we have had four ice Ages in the Northern Hemisphere, known as the Gunz, Mindel, Riss and Wurm, separated by three interglacial periods. Each glacial period was interrupted a number of times by a period of ameliorated conditions. The Wurm Ice Age had two such periods of slight improvement of the climate. We are now in the Flandrian - either the fourth interglacial or a past glacial period - only time will tell. This post-glacial period began about 10,000 years ago as the ice caps melted.

The Red Moss shows six major assemblages of tree pollen after the improvement from the first tundra type vegetation following the slow change in the climate and the gradual movement of the ice sheet north. These are:

a. A birch, pine, juniper period. About 10,000 to 9,500 years before the present. Birch is the dominant pollen type with considerable poplar and willow. Grasses and *Cyperaceae (the Sedge family)* are the dominant herb vegetation.
b. A birch, pine, hazel period. About 10,000 to 8,800 before the present. Juniper and willow decline and grasses and Cyperaceae remain dominant herbs
c. Hazel, pine period. About 8,800 to 8,200 before present. This period is marked by the arrival of the first elm and oak pollen.
d. Pine, hazel and elm period. About 8,200 to 7,100 before present. Birch declines and pine becomes dominant with elm exceeding oak.
e. Oak, elm, alder period. About 7,100 to 5,000 before present. Birch and pine decline and alder increases dramatically. Lime and ash become common and ericaceous pollen is present in large amounts.

f.   Oak, alder period. About 5,000 before present to the present day. Elm, lime and ash decline and oak becomes dominant. There is a marked increase in pollen from plants of open and disturbed land such as Nettles, Dock, Ribwort Plantain, and compositae such as Artemesia and Wild Chamomile.

Note that the above dates are derived from radiocarbon dating and are necessarily approximations.

Man, 10,000 years before the present, was still in the Palaeolithic or Old Stone Age and had little impact, as a hunter-gatherer, on his environment. It was only about 5,000 years before present that man entered his Neolithic stage and slowly introduced farming and stock rearing. The Bronze Age began roughly 4,000 years before the present and so, with improved axes, did the felling of trees and the slow clearance of the forests. This accelerated with the coming of the Iron Age, about 2,500 years before the present, and the combination of a slowly increasing human population with increased tree felling and increased grazing intensity from domestic stock, reduced tree seedling regeneration, and led to the treeless moors now so familiar to us".

Robert Yates.

+++

Anyone any information about this?

I received the following email from Alan Foster of Atherton who wrote:

"I grew up in Smithills Bolton as a kid and remember seeing a map once, that showed a tunnel starting in the hill at the top of Smithills Dean Road and exiting at the back of Belmont Road.

If I remember correctly, it was a pretty straight tunnel, we were going to investigate it at one point but never got fully round to it."

Is there anyone else out there that can throw any light whatsoever on this tunnel as I have never come across it before. Although I was aware of the coal mines up on Smithills Moor I've never seen any maps of diagrams of any locations nor have I met anyone who remembers any open drift entrances.

If anyone can help ..... please get in touch : d.lane@btinternet.com

Interesting and attractive map of the panoramic view from Winter Hill can be found at: http://www.viewfinderpanoramas.org/panoramas/ENG/Winter.gif

Coal Seams on Winter Hill.

As mentioned earlier, there are two major coal seams on Winter Hill which were widely exploited. They were known as the Upper Mountain Mine and the Lower Mountain Mine.

There are however other coal seams in the locality and several of the outcrops can be clearly seen on the surface. One to outcrop right next to the road, can be found in the stream by the side of the Rivington to Belmont road about 200 yards past the Moses Cocker farmhouse. The coal seam can be seen jutting out from the bank at water level about 10 yards from where the stream passes beneath the road. There are at least two further coal outcrops further up the valley. According to some geology books there were levels in the stream banks to extract the coal. These are all part of the Holcombe Brook Coal Seam which is also known as the Margery Mine.

On Rivington Moor and Smithills Moor, lie the Sand Rock Mine Coal seams which formed a "double seam". These seams plus the associated fireclay were extensively used in the Horwich area in the stone-ware industry.

South of Belmont village can be found the Brooksbottoms Coal seam. I presume it is the Brooksbottoms seam that was worked in the Shaly Dingle (see an earlier article) area near the main Belmont Road.

There are other coal seams - but they're so thin they're not worth mentioning!

The panoramic view below is courtesy and copyright of Jonathan de Ferranti at: http://www.viewfinderpanoramas.org/

188

TEENAGERS SAFE AFTER MINE ORDEAL

By CLIVE NAISH

SIX Lancashire teenagers were rescued by Coal Board safety men early today after a 13-hour ordeal in a disused coal mine near Chorley.

The six, four boys and two girls, were safe but frightened. They took only a torch, a cigarette lighter and an apple with them on their adventure.

A police spokesman said: "What a survival kit! They are lucky to be alive."

The six were: Janet Fishwick, 13, Brazley Avenue, Horwich; Mark Wilkes, 14, Chorley New Road, Horwich; Lester Pearson, 14, Panton Street, Horwich; John Anthony, 14, Sefton Lane, Horwich; Patricia Quilliam, 15, Brazley Avenue, Horwich and Anthony Stott, 14, Beech Avenue, Horwich.

It was 2 pm yesterday when eight youngsters crawled through a three-feet wide hole into the disused Winter Hill Mine at Rivington, near Chorley. The hole had been closed but re-opened by rains.

Two turned back but the other six went on to explore old workings which run for miles.

The two who turned back told their parents and when the six had been underground for six hours they were reported missing.

Police called out an NCB rescue team which toiled in the night and brought the youngsters to the surface and safety early today.

One of the girls trapped spoke today of her 13-hour ordeal.

Thirteen-year-old Janet Fishwick, was one of six people who got stuck in the old mine shaft when they went exploring on an afternoon's ramble.

They were rescued from the mine shaft on Wilderswood Moors at 1 40 am this morning after a massive rescue operation had been launched by police from the Lancashire and Greater Manchester forces who also called in a mine rescue team.

Janet who attends Rivington and Blackrod High School said as she was comforted by her father today: "We were just walking round and round in circles, and in the end just decided to sit down, huddle together and keep each other warm. All we had was one torch and an apple.

"It was frightening. We just hoped that somebody would come and find us. Everybody was asleep except me when I thought I heard something. I woke them up but they said I was hearing things. Then we heard somebody shouting as we shouted back. We were all so relieved. It was very cold."

RAMBLE

The group of teenagers set off for an afternoon's ramble which turned into a nightmare. The alarm was raised by Patricia Quilliam's brother Mark and Peter Elliot, of Brunswick Avenue, Horwich, when the teenagers failed to return home. Tanker driver William Fishwick and his son - in - law John Hurst, of Derwent Close, Horwich, were first on the hillside when they became worried after Janet had failed to come home for tea.

"We went up first but didn't have any proper clothing on and so came back," said Mr Fishwick. "We went up again and went into the cave and started shouting but nobody could hear us."

The rescue team from Boothstown, near Manchester, were then called in and warned civilians to keep out of the old mine workings because of the possibility of dangerous gas. While police and rescue workers awaited the arrival of the pit rescue team searchlights were set up and the mine workings sealed off.

Police were led by Supt Ian Hunter.

The teenagers were found soon after the pit rescue team entered the workings and after a check at Bolton Royal Infirmary were allowed home at about 3 am this morning.

John Anthony said: "We went in once to explore, but came out to go home, but then decided to go back to look at a lake inside. We got to the lake and decided to come out a different way, but got lost, we were going round and round in circles."

Lester Pearson

LANCASHIRE EVENING POST, NOVEMBER 15TH 1976

A view, circa 1905, of George's Lane (as we know it today) under construction. The view is taken soon after passing Sportsman's Cottage heading towards Rivington Pike. Note the "old" moorland road on the left hand side of the picture.

Photo above shows exactly the same view today!

More stone axes!

And yet ANOTHER stone axe has been found in the area to add to the two already found on Winter Hill. The latest find is shown above and was found in April 2006 by Ian Harper on the banks of Anglezarke Reservoir near to the Waterman's Cottage.

It is a highly polished axe, posssibly intended for ritual or ornamental purposes and is in near perfect condition except for one small chip which can be seen near the bottom edge. The tiny flint arrowhead found by myself (and illustrated earlier in this book) was found within a mile of the axe .... so who knows what else is lying there to be found. Needless to say, if you DO make any new finds in the area PLEASE let me know so that we can ALL share in the history of our area.

++

The Horwich Borehole.

Whilst walking around the lower flanks of Winter Hill, especially in the stream valleys, those of us who like looking at rocks are often aware that the nature and of the fabric of the rocks changes when we are heading either up or down the hill. Some rocks are grey and fine grained, others have a very rough texture and are large grained

The different permutations seem endless, and the sheer variety of rocks over fairly small distances often surprises some people. Different layers of rocks were formed at different periods of time. Most of the Winter Hill rocks were formed (or "laid down") around 300 million years ago. The different layers were formed in differing "environments". Some were laid down in fast moving water, some in stagnant swamp-like conditions etc. Most (but not all) of these different layers or different types of rock have been given names such as "Haslingden Flags" or "Holcomb Brook Grit".

Just across the road from the entrance to Curleys Fisheries (near the bottom of Georges Lane) is a pumping station hidden in the bushes. Prior to this being built, a borehole was drilled to over 1,100 feet to test the rock strata and all the different rock layers were identified and their depths and thicknesses recorded.

Horwich or Ousel Nest Grit	0-90 ft
Margery Flags	124-198 ft
Six Inch Mine Marine Band	at 276 feet
Rough Rock	302-338 ft
Sand Rock Mine Coal seam	at 340 ft
Rough Rock	346-375 ft
Upper Haslingdon Flags	384-624 ft
Haslingden Flag Marine Band	at 730ft
Lower Haslingden Flags	Not found
Holcombe Brook Marine Band	at 860 ft
Holcombe Brook Coal Seam	at 872 ft
Holcombe Brook Grit	884-950 ft
Brooksbottoms Coal Seam	at 979 ft
Brooksbottoms Grit	984-1170 ft

The "gaps" in the depths given, are composed of mudstones and shales and do not have any "names".

ANOTHER small free book about Winter Hill now available on the Internet …. "Carboniferous Fossils of Winter Hill and surrounding areas". To download a copy go to

http://www.daveweb.co.uk/whfossil.htm

It is also available in printed book form at:
http://stores.lulu.com/microlight

The Date Stone of Winter Hill.

Boyd Harris brought to my attention a rather strange stone in the Shaley Dingle/Martha Tree Delph area on the Northern flanks of Winter Hill – see the map of the area – the Whimberry Hill area - earlier in this book.

In the earlier article I mentioned the causeway in that area. If you continue walking up the right side of the river, with the causeway on your left (at this point the stream has three tributaries – take the centre one - you will come to a large boulder with 3 dates cut deeply into it. They are 1805, 1912 & 1922. The GPS location is: SD 68144 14356

Has anyone ANY idea what these dates represent? Who might have engraved them? ANY information would be welcomed!

Montcliffe and quarry

Appendix 1

This book contains the research and information compiled by many people. Below is a list of those who have contributed to this publication. In every case where I am aware of the writer, I freely acknowledge use of their work and have mentioned them below. In those cases where I have been able to contact them I give my thanks for their permission to use their work. In those cases where I have been unable to contact the writer (only a couple), I apologise in advance for not consulting with them. If they would care to contact me I will either add their name and reference to this list - or even remove their contribution from the book if this is what they would prefer. As this publication is not "for sale" in any normal fashion, I hope people will not be too offended if their contribution is not acknowledged below or if I have not been able to obtain their prior permission.

My thanks to everyone involved. The names are in no particular order!

D A Owen "Rivington and District before 1066 AD"
H M Ordnance Survey
L H Tonks "Geology of Manchester and S E Lancashire Coalfield"

Paul Baxendale
Ian and Sue Harper
Alf Molyneux
Alan Davies
Mark Wright
Clive Weake
John Bell
Gary Rhodes
Rodney J Ireland "Geological walk on River Douglas north of Horwich"
Bolton Mountain Rescue Team. http://www.boltonmrt.org.uk
Bill Learmouth. TV mast construction photo's + cover photo
British Trust for Conservation Volunteers (North West) http://www.btcv.org/lancashire/front.htm
Dave Healey
Christine Tudor. "Rivington Pike. Erosion Control & Management Plan"
Harry Houghton
T Morris "Rivington Review"
Norman Hoyle. "Reservoirs from Rivington to Rossendale"
Gordon Readyhough
J Rawlinson
Paul Lacey.
Winter Hill Website: http://www.winterhill.org
A O'Rourke
Rivington Soaring Association. http://www.sar.bolton.ac.uk/ian/rsa.htm
Eric Hewis http://www.pbase.com/ezz/image/50313504
David Swain
A O'Rourke

Robert Yates "Past Vegetation, future global warming"
Alan Foster
Ian Duff
Jonathan de Ferranti: http://www.viewfinderpanoramas.org or http://www.viewfinderpanoramas.org/panoramas/ENG/Winter.gif
Boyd Harris
William Kay
Rivington Visitor Centre
Munki

Appendix 2

There are a number of books published which contain information about Winter Hill and it's locality. Below is given a brief list of some of them. If anyone knows the titles and authors of any not listed please get in touch with me (d.lane@btinternet.com) and I'll add them.

M D Smith	Rivington, Lancashire
	Leverhulmes Rivington
	About Horwich
	More about Horwich
	About Anglezarke
P L Watson	Rivington Pike, History & Fell Race
Kenneth Fields	A visitors Guide to Rivington
Gladys Sellers	Walks on the West Pennine Moors
John Rawlinson	About Rivington
Norman Hoyle Rossendale	Reservoirs from Rivington to
George Birtill	The Enchanted Hills
	Heather in my hat.

John Dixon & Jaana Jarvinen.   Walks around the West Pennine Moors

Norman Hoyle Rossendale   Reservoirs from Rivington to

David Holding	Murder in the Heather (published in 1991 by The Friends of Smithills Hall)
Robin Smith	"Smithills Moor & Two Lads" (Halliwell Local History Society) "Two Lads, My theory"
Paul Salveson	"Will yo' come o' Sunday Morning"

Also by the author:

Winter Hill Scrapbook

Deep Sky Objects in Canes Venatici

Astley Green Colliery

Photographic catalogue of deep sky objects in the Canes Venatici constellation.

Carboniferous Fossils of Winter Hill & surrounding areas

Pit Brow Lasses Scrapbook

Palestinians – the forgotten people.

Wet Earth Scrapbook

Isn't religion weird – Quotations for Atheists!

Photographic Guide to Ursa Major using the Sloan Digital Survey Telescope.

Most of the above are available free of charge on the internet via www.d.lane.btinternet.co.uk

Some of the titles are available in paperback book format at **http://stores.lulu.com/microlight**

....